FABRIC PICTURES

By the same author

ART FOR YOUNG PEOPLE

in collaboration with Bernard Carter

I *Owl and Moths:* by Margaret Kaye

FABRIC PICTURES

BY

EUGENIE ALEXANDER

MILLS & BOON LIMITED

17-19 FOLEY STREET LONDON W1A 1DR

First Published 1959
Second Edition 1963
Reprinted 1965
Third Edition 1967
Reprinted 1968
Reprinted 1972
© Eugenie Carter 1959
New material in this edition, © Eugenie Carter 1967

ISBN 0 263 69998 6

PRINTED IN GREAT BRITAIN BY
BIDDLES LTD., GUILDFORD, SURREY

Contents

List of Illustrations

COLOUR PLATES

HALF-TONE PLATES

Acknowledgements

I SHOULD like to express my thanks to the many people who helped me in various ways during the course of the preparation of this book, including:

Everyone who has given me permission to reproduce their pictures.

Assistance given from the staff and the loan of a machine from Jones Sewing Machine Co. Ltd.

Assistance given from the staff and the loan of machines from Singer Sewing Machine Co.

Assistance given by Copydex.

Barbara J. Morriss, Department of Circulation at the Victoria and Albert Museum.

Mr Delbanco for information and assistance.

The Embroiderers' Guild for assistance and the provision of photographs.

Mr Zika Ascher and his staff for assistance.

Photographers: Ellis Sykes and Gordon McLeish (colour plates), Alexander Hedderwick, W. Churcher, George Parmiter, R. F. Wills, Joseph McKenzie, Edward Leigh, Harry Hodson, Kenneth de Dehn, John Bignell.

E. A.

Introduction

FABRIC pictures have come into their own again as a new and exciting art form, and are becoming a very popular means of interior decoration. While retaining their individuality, by reason of the application, piece by piece, of varied materials, they may be compared with stained glass, collage, mosaic and painting.

The contemporary trend, where professional artists design and execute their own work and so achieve a plastic unity of ideas, composition, materials, technique and personal style, has lifted fabric pictures out of the realm of pretty embroidered "cottage pictures". It is increasingly appreciated that works of art can be created from almost any material given the fundamental qualities of good design and respect for the nature of the material used. We live in an age which has accepted the experimental yet constructional view of the Bauhaus, the newspaper collages of Picasso, the wood-strips used in the Braque still-life pictures, and the sand-pictures of the Victorian era (made by a special process from different-coloured grains of sand—the Arthur Jeffress Gallery showed two of these portraying lions and tigers against a jungle background). In an exhibition, "Pictures without Paint", at the Artists' International Association Gallery, there were examples of works made from such substances as wire, glass, sacking, plastics, perspex, metal and plaster. A delightful figure study by BAJ was made with a background of pink patterned furnishing fabric and orange canvas. The hair was made of twisted straw and the eyes and nose were chunks of glass.

Someone said to me the other day, "I was rather put off appliqué pictures when I was at school because I associated them with bits of felt painstakingly button-holed round the edge and found it rather boring, but the way it's done nowadays makes one want to sit down and make a picture straightaway." Many people, having seen examples at art galleries, on television and in women's magazines, have experimented on their own and have derived endless pleasure from the process. This book has been written in order to fill in the gaps and give more of the necessary detailed information so that the best possible effects can be achieved. The appeal of the medium lies in the fact that it is not necessary to be an exquisite needle-woman or an artist in order to make a picture. The textures, colours and patterns of the endless choice of contemporary fabrics often suggest a subject, and there are few women who cannot cut out simple shapes with a pair of scissors. There are so many things around us which provide ideas that there is no need to resort to the old overworked designs of hollyhocks and crinolines. There is no need either to stick to any hard-and-fast rules—experiment is the keynote.

Pictures can be made by sticking on pieces of fabric with a rubber solution which will not stain the material. For those who love embroidery the pieces can be stitched by hand, using as many or as few stitches as they please. Times have changed since everything was laboriously filled in with satin stitch. It is also possible to use any type of sewing machine, hand, foot-treadle or electric. It does not matter if there are no special gadgets for varying stitch design; even on an old-fashioned machine a variety of line, colour and pattern can be obtained. Indeed, sometimes it is an asset to have limitations. Too many varieties of decorative stitches used without discrimination can look vulgar, like some of the dreadful examples seen on the cheaper skirts and dresses on show in the windows of so many shopping centres, which are not helped by the mundane designs churned out so unimaginatively. It is always best to ponder over the stitches first and see whether they fulfil their purpose or whether a simple running stitch would have done as well. Simple but sophisticated designs which reflect the age we live in can be achieved by these mechanical means.

When I first started machine embroidery on my grandmother's early Singer hand model (which is now over 60 years old and had a special box made for it so that it could be carried on the backs of elephants and camels abroad), my husband, whose only acquaintance with it was when he oiled it occasionally for me, thought that he would like to try it. He started with a rush of enthusiasm, the stitching careering round faces, birds and leaves, all in a mad jumble. As an artist he was delighted to be "drawing" in a new medium.

A combination of hand and machine work can give pleasant results, the freedom, neatness and precision of the pen-like running lines of a sewing machine contrasting with the heavier effects of hand embroidery. Merely looking at various fabrics and juggling them about can lead to a greater knowledge of colour and texture, which can contribute towards enriching everyday life.

From the Old Testament days and from the time of the Siege of Troy down to the present, women have made wall-hangings and pictures. In the ancient East they adorned the tents for the men. In medieval homes and churches, the needle, the brush and the chisel taught morality, religion and love by way of pictorial symbolism.

Fabric-picture-making is becoming a popular lesson in schools. I was talking recently to a mother who was helping her 11-year-old child with "a clown", which was her homework. She found part of an old sheet for the background, which she dyed with cold water dye, odds and ends of old dress materials, some pieces of lace and ric-rac, and a broken string of beads. She became so fascinated that she cut out hands for the clown and would have gone on but the child reminded her that she was meant to do it on her own!

The therapeutic value of the medium with its natural instinctive appeal and its accent on colour and texture, was brought home to me when I received a letter from a mother whose 10-year-old daughter had watched a children's television programme dealing with a fabric-picture competition. The girl, who had had polio, had lost all interest in creative work, but on seeing the examples shown on the programme she was so bewitched by the pictures the other children had made, and by the materials they had used, that she set to and made a very inventive design herself. She entered this for the competition and then went on to make more.

1 *Europa and the Bull:* by Eugenie Alexander
(*In the collection of Mrs Bryant*)

2 *Tea by the River:* by Eugenie Alexander
(*In the collection of Mrs Cooper*)

An obvious advantage is that the work does not require a room to itself. It can be left at any moment and taken up again easily, as will be seen in the following chapters. Designs can be simple or as complicated as you choose, provided that simplicity does not lead to emptiness or complication to chaos!

To quote from some advice given by Eric Newton on the subject of fabric pictures in *Time and Tide*—"Take advantage of what the medium can do: succumb to its limitations, and a new set of possibilities will arrive of their own accord."

CHAPTER I

History of the Use of Fabric for Pictorial Purposes

FABRICS have played their part in the world since almost the beginning of civilization. Women have always had a natural love of them as they form a background to their lives both in their homes and in their clothes.

The whole process of embroidery was so esteemed by the Romans that they called it "painting with a needle" and it has been said that it claims a place in history before either architecture or sculpture. It is fascinating to trace back the use of fabrics in various pictorial forms. Some people might feel they are not very interested in doing this, but it is very much bound up with the various methods of fabric-picture-making. They may find that descriptions of work from different countries and different centuries will serve to create ideas which could be adapted in a contemporary style for their own pictures.

It is thought that embroidery started from the use of a purely useful stitch ("lacing stitch") with a bone needle to sew up the skins of the animals that were prepared for food, to join up the sides of a tent, and to make seams in clothes. Quite naturally this led to the use of more decorative stitches for clothes; to the use of colours and simple patterns (straight lines, zig-zags, wavy lines, dots) and from there on to a style.

Early forms of appliqué may have arisen from the necessity to patch worn fabrics with whatever material was at hand. The first rough attempts may in themselves have suggested greater possibilities of decoration and later selection of colour and design evolved.

10th century B.C., *Greek*

It was the Greeks who introduced sprays and wreaths of bay, oak, ivy, vines and fruits for embroidery decoration. The Grecian women in Homer's works were all artists with the needle. It is believed that his descriptions of beautiful dresses and furnishings were derived from his knowledge of Babylonian embroideries. From him we hear that the goddess Pallas Athene patronized the craft of embroidery. She was always seen in embroidered garments which she worked and wove with her own hands. The sacred peplos which robed her statue was renewed every four years. Noble maidens embroidered it with a representation of the battle of gods and giants and it was then carried like a flag in procession through the city. On one occasion Pallas Athene was challenged to an embroidery contest by a mortal maiden named Arachne, one of her former pupils. She was defeated and was so angry with the girl that she struck her on the head. Arachne, who had a very sensitive nature, was so hurt by this indignity that she hung herself in despair and was changed by Athene into a spider.

The patience of Penelope, wife of Odysseus, is an example to all who dislike unpicking their work. She promised her unwanted suitors that she would marry one of them as soon as she had finished a robe she was making, and then to gain time she secretly undid at night what she had done in the day.

In one of Homer's stories he describes Helen's golden spindle which could only produce perfect thread. (The ancient sun-worshippers thought that gold had a magical value in whatever form it was used and they ascribed to it the life-giving power of the sun). There is a description of her giving her work to Telemachus— "Helen, the fair lady, stood by the coffer wherein were her robes of curious needle-work which she herself had wrought. Then Helen, the fair lady, lifted it out, the widest and most beautifully embroidered of all, and it shone like a star. This she sent as a gift to his future wife."

5th century B.C., *Scythian*

Richly embroidered hangings with gold plaques sewn on in the shape of flowers were found in the magnificent tombs where Scythian chieftains were buried.

1st century A.D., *Egyptian*

The ancient Egyptians formed a patchwork funeral tent for their queen out of multi-coloured goatskins in geometrical patterns and with primitive symbols of wings and the papryus and lotus flowers they loved so much. In Egypt linen sails on trading vessels had embroidered designs on them. They must have appeared like giant samplers or glorified patchwork flapping in the wind. So that their emblems would be easily recognized by trading merchants, the stitching was taken right through the material and the pattern duplicated on the other side, portraying rows of birds, flowers and abstract patterns. The boats of Antony and Cleopatra had brilliant purple sails and this colour was exclusive to the admiral.

1st century, *Chinese*

A Chinese quilted carpet which was actually found on the floor of a tomb was worked all over with a bold pattern of large spirals. These were a world-wide symbol rarely absent from Chinese art. The border was composed of a series of animal motifs and a symbolic tree. Two groups of animals in combat in applied cloth of purple, brown and white were outlined in twisted thread forming a cord. The quilting was coarse and only sufficient to keep the layers of material in place.

5th century, *Byzantine*

One of the early Byzantine embroideries of Christ and his disciples, used for religious instruction as most of the people could neither read nor write, had a background laid with silver threads over a double thread of string padding. The flesh

3 *The Fish:* by Eugenie Alexander

and draperies were embroidered with flat stitching in untwisted silk. Faces were worked in horizontal stitching, which was taken over fine cords to make contours, and the draperies were outlined with silver thread over string padding, the whole presenting a rich raised effect.

6th century, Coptic

Some of the Coptic tapestries give an impression of a needlework execution to anyone who is unacquainted with the capacity of the weaver's tools and the use of the free shuttle. There are among the examples in the Victoria and Albert Museum two delightful designs. One is a brown bird with a red beak and legs (a linen and wool tapestry woven on one woollen warp applied to linen cloth) and the other an Egyptian head in yellow, orange, brown and pink (wool tapestry woven on one woollen warp).

8th century, Chinese

Both in China and Japan the arts of embroidery and painting were regarded on equal terms. It is thought that the lustrous brilliance of the printed and dyed silks greatly influenced early painters. The effects achieved by couching flat strips of gold on to material with silk thread were copied in painting by the application of gold by special inlaid method.

The similarity to painting is very marked in some of the embroidered pictures found in the temples from the caves of the Thousand Buddhas. The British Museum has one which is 9 feet high, representing a life-size image of the Buddha. He is in a light green robe with a mantle in tones of red, and is standing on a lotus flower between two of his disciples (dressed as monks with shaved heads and haloes) and two Bodhisattvas. On either side of him, at the top are Apsaras (water-nymphs) on clouds. The spiral effect of the design is very marked. Above the Buddha's head is a rich canopy decorated with a jewelled chain and tassels. At the bottom of the picture are kneeling donors and two seated lions. (This brings to mind later religious paintings specially commissioned by wealthy patrons who were included in the pictures bearing offerings to God, the Virgin Mary and the saints.) There is no black in the picture—the colours used are light and dark blue, yellow, pink, grey and dark brown. The embroidery is worked through two layers of material, a fine buff silk mounted on a coarse linen for additional strength, with thread which is equivalent to modern "floss". The stitches used are mostly "satin" and "long and short", with a few portions in "chain stitch" and "split stitch". The work was started by following along the contours with indigo-coloured stitching and then working inwards. There is slight variation on the folds of the drapery—the stitches here are coarser than those on the larger masses. The features are delicately modelled in "split stitch" which is suggestive of the *Opus Anglicanum* (English Church embroidery) of 13th and 14th centuries.

11th century, English

The Bayeux Tapestry, one of the greatest and most famous of existing embroideries, has been described as a "diary written with a needle". It shows various scenes illustrating the Norman Conquest by means of picture stories with subtitles surrounded by borders which include birds and animals. One part of the design shows Edward seated on his throne in the castle, bidding farewell to Harold. Another shows a woman and child fleeing from a burning house with a Latin inscription saying "Here a house is burned". The linen strip background is just over 230 feet long and about 20 inches wide. The work is done in wool inlaid work and outline stitch, and the colours used are chiefly blue, red, yellow, green, black and grey.

12th century, English

The crusaders carried their own pictures with them in the form of applied shapes of birds and beasts on their armorial bearings. These identified them in battle.

In many medieval works spaces were left open in the weaving for figures of the saints to be inserted by inlaid appliqué. Spaces were also sometimes left for faces and hands only, and these were then painted.

14th century, English

In the British Museum there is a panel of silk embroidery illustrating Christ and his disciples. It is worked in fine split stitch (which gives the particularly accurate and delicate drawing required) mainly in blue, grey and biscuit on a laid gold ground. The very fine stitching and manner of working has led to bulging in parts. This circumstance gave rise to the opinion that hot irons were used to model the faces.

15th century, Italian

Botticelli realized the decorative qualities of Armenian work and persuaded the Church to use it for religious depiction on banners and curtains. It also had the advantage of taking less time and material than pure embroidery and tapestry.

16th century, English

Panels depicted biblical or classical subjects, the characters in contemporary dress appearing against a garden background. Queen Elizabeth's ladies-in-waiting made a bed-cover for her with motifs of pears on trees. These were appliquéd with buttonhole stitch. At Hardwick Hall there can still be seen large wall-hangings in velvet and gold (it is believed the pieces used were from old vestments and copes) illustrating the "virtues". Mary Queen of Scots embroidered a design in tent stitch on canvas while she was a prisoner at Hardwick. Perhaps the galaxy of roses, thistles, lilies, birds and beasts which she worked (illustrating *Aesop's Fables*) helped her to forget her surroundings.

17th century, Swiss

In Switzerland, hanging wall pockets were in use in the 17th century. One of them, made to celebrate a wedding, was in fine-coloured silks on a blue silk background. It was 30 inches high and divided into five like the divisions of a sampler. The first pocket showed a figure between two pairs of winged mermaids holding hearts. The second showed an angel with the coats-of-arms of the bride's and groom's families on either side. The other pockets showed symbolic figures representing Wisdom, Charity, Hospitality, Truth, and Justice in the dress of the period and placed beside large sprays of flowers tied with ribbon.

17th century, English

Early pattern books were used as aids by embroideresses. They were very expensive and had a limited life because designs were traced by pricking through each page of the book on to a cloth underneath. Charcoal or coloured powder was then rubbed through the holes. Other sources of design were woodcuts and engravings in contemporary herbals and bestiaries.

In 1640, John Taylor, the water poet, wrote a long introductory poem to pattern books for embroidery, "The Needles Excellency". Part of it mentions favourite motifs of the time:

> Flowers, Plants and Fishes; Beasts, Birds, Flyes and Bees,
> Hills, Dales, Plains, Pastures, Skies, Seas, Rivers, Trees,
> There's nothing ne'er at hand or farthest sought,
> But with the needle may be shap'd or wrought.

Needlework pictures also became popular and hung in the small panels which lined the walls. They were executed in tent stitch on canvas and often designed from contemporary engravings. One small unfinished piece was a garden scene which shows the careful tracing of the forms to be embroidered. There were many portraits of Charles I worked on canvas in wool, often with silk used for highlights and with the needlepoint lace of the period very carefully imitated.

"A Lady in the reign of Charles I" is a delightful portrait worked on white satin. Her features are outlined and only the hair, eyes and mouth are in solid shading. The ear-rings and necklace are padded. A house and garden are in the background and a wreath makes a vignette round them all. This is made from small loops of parchment wrapped round with hair-like green floss silk which alternates with strips of braid made from plaited gimp. The whole stands up stiffly like leaves.

Stump work, in which portions of the design were padded to give a high-relief, three-dimensional effect, was extremely popular from about 1625 to the end of the century and was used to decorate caskets, looking-glass frames and bookbindings. The style of work originated after the raised ecclesiastical embroideries from Italy and Germany which were done in the 15th and 16th centuries. Motifs chosen in stump work were scenes from the Old Testament or mythical characters in Stuart

II *The Park*: by Eugenie Alexander
(In the collection of Dr and Mrs Barrie Jay)

costume. The figures of Charles I and Henrietta Maria were often included, tents (in high relief and showing folds), apples, pears, wonderful lions, parakeets, butter-flies and roses; a gay galaxy of colour, sumptuousness and a charming disregard for reality, emphasized by the strange proportions of the objects. The parts which were to be in high relief were worked separately on pieces of stout linen stretched on a frame and were applied to the background when completed. The design was sketched on to the linen, then the shape was padded with hair or wool and this was kept secure by crossed threads in lattice-work formation, supplying the raised foundation or "stump". The latter was then covered with close lace stitches and pieces of silk or satin, which were in turn covered with embroidery in long and short stitch. Paper was then pasted at the back to stop the possibility of frayed or loosened edges. The design was afterwards cut out and fastened in its proper place, which had been drawn out on the silk, satin or canvas background. Gimp, couching or fine cord hid the outlines where the "stump" work had been attached. Sometimes carved wood was used for heads, hands and figures. This in turn was covered with pieces of satin, silk or a close network of lace-stitch. Real hair was often used and the eyes and mouth were painted or embroidered. The ruffles were usually done separately in needlepoint lace stitches which were closely and heavily worked, using fine wire round the edges for stiffening so that they would stand away from the background when they were fastened on to the figures. Sprigs of artificial flowers were used, beads for eyes, seed pearls for costumes, bits of paste, glass and metal spangles.

Large wall-hangings portraying country scenes in wool and silk were also popular. The ladies of the family worked at them on canvas in tent-stitch in great and pro-longed industry, and the finished products were fastened flat upon the walls with a wooden framework. Pepys mentions this in his diary: "Home to my poor wife, who works all day like a horse, at the making of her hangings for our chamber and bed."

18th century, English

Map samplers, darning samplers and cross-stitch samplers with pious texts enclosed in decorative borders were seen everywhere. There were samplers for funeral cards, samplers dealing with life and death, samplers with illustrated prayers, lists of duties to parents and references to virtue, wealth, vice and poverty. Young children were usually given these texts to work on, both to test their skill and help their knowledge. One can imagine the feelings of a 7-year-old girl who had to embroider the following:

> And now my soul another year
> Of thy short life is past
> I cannot long continue here
> And this may be my last.

On the other hand, a pictorial conception of her family and home in the form of a sampler must have provided some amusement and satisfaction to another little girl of 7. This picture was carried out mostly in greens and blues. The border is of delightful stylized trees. At the top is the house surrounded by trees, birds and butterflies; in one corner is a boy with his tutor; in the other are two servants, one of whom is coloured and in charge of the dog. Next comes another pattern of stylized trees and under it the family. Her father, in a blue coat, white stockings and buckled shoes, is pointing to her mother who wears a hooped dress. The five girls play round their parents. After another division of trees there follows a stylized sea filled with mermaids and alligators, with black swans and rare birds near by. This is the faraway land across the seas which the father had obviously visited and where he had probably procured the negro servant. Beneath this are two soldiers in the uniforms of George III.

At the Paris exhibition a curious example from England was the Prince of Wales's pavilion made with various appliqué material. It consisted of a series of Chinese fowling scenes. The human figures were clothed in silk and velvet, the animals were in their own furs, and the birds were made out of the appropriate feathers.

Ribbon work was a pretty picture fashion. Narrow coloured ribbons were used for bouquets of flowers and stiffish coloured muslins or gauze were gathered into petals. Stems and parts of the leaves were in chenille, and French knots formed the flower centres. The flower spray was worked on a rich background such as white satin, and the smaller flowers were embroidered.

Silk pictures were worked in bright flat silk embroidery, either over printed engravings or on to underlying painted silk or satin fabric. Sometimes these designs were sold with the pastoral backgrounds, skies and faces ready painted and all that was required was satin stitch for jackets and gowns and French knots for the sheep.

In their leisure time at sea, sailors worked gay and ornate pictures in wools and silks. These were usually of sailing ships and full of exuberant fancies.

Other pictures in fine black silk were executed in a method known as "hair" embroidery because of the incredible likeness of the stitches to the engraved line. Many of them were imitations of engravings from *The Cries of London*.

Then there were the astonishing, slavish copies of famous oil paintings which, quite ignoring the vastly different medium, were worked in coloured wools to as close an imitation of the original as was possible. Miss Linwood was the most famous exponent of this strange art. She had many exhibitions of her work and the Society for the Encouragement of the Arts gave her a medal for "excellent imitations of pictures in Needlework". Reviews mentioned that the richness of her colouring not only competed with that of the great oil-painters but, in some instances, her copies were more admired than their originals! Her "pictures in worsted" were worked in softly coloured wools using long-and-short stitch and satin stitch haphazard. She began to embroider at 13 and did her last picture when she was 75. Specially prepared cloth was woven for her. She had her own ideas about colour and her threads were specially dyed. She regarded embroidery as a "sister art of painting" and refused £3,000 for her copy of "Salvator Mundi" (from the original by Carlo Dolci) which she bequeathed to Queen Victoria.

Thomas Stevens wove silk pictures on a specially adapted loom. These were woven in a continuous repeat of one design with space left between each so that the pictures could be cut apart for mounting. Gay glossy silks were used for the major figures, and threads were manipulated to catch the light at different angles. These contrasted effectively with a matt background and viewed from a distance looked like water-colour paintings. The artists who designed these pictures centred the chief interest on the foregrounds to get over the difficulties of achieving three-dimensional effects. Early pictures were small enough to be enclosed in letters for birthdays and other celebrations. Subjects chosen for framing were portraits, historical scenes (such as the Lady Godiva procession at Coventry with details of houses, crowds, horses, flags and banners), architectural scenes, sports (including cycling, rowing, coursing, steeple-chasing, hunting, racing and cricket), scenes from contemporary life and miniature copies of contemporary paintings.

18th century, French

Several different forms of pictures made from fabric became very popular. In France, the artists Boucher and Watteau produced designs with heathen gods, cupids, garlands and floating ribbons, which were well suited to tapestry and embroidery.

Many religious silk pictures, which were often mistaken for needlework, were produced at the convent of St. Elmo by the monks. Often the silk threads were laid down and attached to the background by a gum made from shellac. In one example, the saint's hands, head and feet were painted on silk, the clouds, trees, ground and the saint's clothing were done in an imitation satin stitch, while two angels were stuck on to the silk background.

18th century, Italian

From Italy came the idea of embroidering on paper in floss silks. These were carefully worked so that both sides were alike and were called "colifichet". Designs were either of sacred subjects or flowers in vases. When finished they were placed between two pieces of glass.

18th century, Chinese

In Chinese hanging pictures silk was stretched across a frame. A design, which was commonly a landscape with trees, blossoms, fruit, birds and figures, was drawn and then worked by a person on each side pushing the needle through the material from one to the other.

19th century, American

Patchwork quilts were very popular. One in the collection of the Victoria and Albert Museum has a "Persian palm lily" pattern used as a "repeat" motif. It is a stylized, bold, flat design of flowers, leaves and berries in a vase and is made up of

5 *Wartime Winter*: by Ellen Hallett
(*In the collection of Donald Hughes, Esq.*)

4 *Spring*: by Ellen Hallett

cloth applied on a linen ground. The edges are buttonholed and there is a small amount of embroidered detail.

19th century, German

In 1804, a Berlin print-seller, George Philipson, introduced Berlin wool-work pictures. Designs were produced on squared paper so that the embroideress could copy them in cross-stitch on a similarly squared open-meshed canvas simply by counting the stitches. Here again little sense of relationship between design and material was shown. One design was Landseer's "Mary Queen of Scots mourning over the Dying Douglas". Silks and beads were also introduced later but originally only the bright rich-coloured wools dyed in Berlin were used. This work was used for chair seats and cushions as well as for pictures. In 1810, a Berlin needlewoman, Frau Wittich, and her husband, a print-seller, persuaded artists to invent or copy patterns for prints which were pasted on to felt and then embroidered. Felt, which had been painted in a darker grey in places to give a shadowed effect, was used for a picture of an urn in "Homage to Shakespeare", showing Mrs. Siddons taking flowers to a memorial. Everything else, except for the coloured engraved head and hands, was done in satin stitch. In a more unusual picture of Elizabeth I, a black-and-white engraving has been cut away to leave only the outlines of folds of the dress and sleeves, and a piece of tapestry which has a small pattern on it has been stuck behind to show through these openings.

19th century, Caucasian

A fine example of a Caucasian wall panel (approximately 6 by 5 feet) had navy-blue felt for a background with the shapes of birds, animals, people and trees cut out of it and then coral-red, white and pale green pieces had been placed behind the spaces. They were securely attached to the background with couched fine white cord. A border of birds and leaves surrounded the inner section which was made up of rectangles of different sizes showing such biblical stories as Adam and Eve, Rebecca at the Well and the Last Supper. There is a delightful panel showing half-views of tigers and lions peeping behind a wall which lies flat on its side with no attempt at perspective.

19th century, English

The Pollock toy theatre publishers introduced tinsel pictures or "patch portraits". These were issued in the form of prints and were decorated by the purchasers by sticking on bits of silk, satin, coloured paper, feathers or tinsels. One typical picture represents the hero in a theatrical stance brandishing his weapons. There were standardized tinsels for special prints which could be bought quite cheaply, "stick-on" ornaments of coloured metal foil, plumes, rosettes, stars, spangles, helmets, and daggers embossed and backed with paper. One print of Napoleon showed him wearing a green silk coat with tinsel medals. Behind him were soldiers on horseback in their original coloured engraved state.

20th century, French

Jean Lurçat has made a great contribution to the design of tapestries. He wanted a "more architectural means of expression than was to be found in easel painting", so he turned to tapestry and the discipline which it imposes, having already a knowledge of embroidering in petit point. He has discovered that a design only lives by strong values in juxtaposition forming definite contrasts. Too many colours at once cancel themselves out. He works out designs using between twenty and forty hues, which might include five shades of yellow going from light to dark. These are all numbered in their appropriate sections and traced from a black and white cartoon which he prepares, thus ensuring that the truest interpretation will be achieved by the craftsmen. The exact character of hatchings, lines and dots to be placed in the various shapes are also indicated by signs. All his work is stimulating and has a vibrancy about it. One tapestry, featuring a cockerel's head, shows the bird (which he saw in a meadow with the sun's rays shining fiercely upon it) with the head, looking like a helmet, executed in short curved contrasting lines. The eye is like a ball of fire and the feathers down the neck can be compared with spiky fishbones. The body is made up of long and short flame-like patterning. The leaves beside him have the same jagged quality. When Jean Lurçat originally saw the cockerel he was impressed by its overwhelming pride and the effect of the sun's rays lighting up its whole body, making it into a kind of red god.

20th century, English

In the 1920's, an artist and teacher, Rebecca Crompton, encouraged an interest in hand and machine embroidered pictures, and this was furthered by the Needlework Development scheme. When the latter ceased to exist some of their works were passed on to the Embroiderer's Guild.

Fabric collage has been playing a very large part in church design—one of the largest commissions, a reredos, was designed and carried out by David Holt (in the workshop of Gerald Hutton) for the church of Our Lady of the Assumption in Albuquerque, New Mexico. It is made up of separate panels 4 feet high by 3 feet wide, 117 in all, to cover an area measuring 40 feet square. Each panel was to be stretched on a wooden frame and set into a large grille to the rear of the altar. White heavy linen formed the background and thousands of pieces of silk, brocade, nylon, net, and 22-carat gold, and silver leaf on kid leather were applied. Fifty miles of cotton were used and details of drawing were added with thick wool and also "drawn" direct with large sewing machines for the finer details. The theme is the Eucharist and the panels depict a large open-work cross, with illustrations from the Old and New Testaments among the motifs.

1966 was a year marking two major fabric collage events in the form of the Embroiderers' Guild Diamond Jubilee and the Ascher Award for the best work of art (in collage and sculpture) utilizing fabric. Reports on these exhibitions are in Chapter VI.

CHAPTER II

How to Make Fabric Pictures

ALWAYS work in a good light with the light coming from over your shoulder on to the materials. At night a daylight bulb is kinder to the colours and the eyes. Get the maximum enjoyment from fabric-picture-making by sitting comfortably and not in a hunched up position as this leads to undue fatigue.

MATERIALS REQUIRED

1 Box or scrapbook for collecting references.
2 H.B. pencil or water-colour brush and box of water-colours, Indian ink, for mapping out preliminary ideas.
3 Rubber.
4 Ruler for measuring picture size, etc.
5 Cartridge paper for making preliminary drawing or painting.
6 Sketchbook to make record of ideas.
7 Drawing pins for pinning paper and stretching.
8 Coloured paper or newspaper for cutting out preliminary ideas.
9 Imperial drawing board for drawing on and for stretching out material (alternatively, any flat surface such as an old table).
10 Set-square, to make certain that the picture is square at the corners.
11 Tracing paper or greaseproof paper for tracing shapes from original plan.
12 Scissors—sharp and pointed, any convenient size.
13 Iron and ironing board for pressing.
14 Ironing cloth to put over materials when puckered.
15 Firm fabrics suitable for backgrounds such as linen, cotton, felt, wool, mattress ticking.
16 Small pieces of muslin, lawn, organdie, cambric, gingham, linen, rayon, nylon, silk, chiffon, velvet, corduroy, velveteen, wool, net, felt, crêpe-de-Chine.
17 A selection of raffia, string, Clark's Anchor stranded cottons, crochet wool, wools, slub yarn, Lurex non-tarnishing metallic yarn, real silk.
18 A selection of braids, ribbons, lace, fringes, cords, ric-rac, sequins, beads, pearls, buttons.
19 Domestic sewing machine for machine embroidery.
20 Needles—a selection of chenille needles (for heavy embroidery) and crewel needles (for fine embroidery). Rustproof pins.
21 Rubber solution (non-staining) for sticking pieces.

22   Orange stick to use with rubber solution.
23   Thimble—silver is better than plastic.
24   Embroidery frame—rectangular, or hoop of convenient size, or an old picture frame can also be used. Material should be wound round the wood structure and the background fabric is basted on securely, retaining a flat, taut surface for working upon. This is not vital and many people work without one.
25   Several sheets of white blotting paper for stretching. This is placed in layers and damped.
26   Stout linen thread for mounting.
27   A frame with glass (to protect materials from the dust). Mount if desired.
28   White cardboard for mounting. Brown is unsuitable and takes the colour out of some of the materials.

HOW TO MAKE A PICTURE—(A) BY HAND

It might be advisable to decide upon a subject which will give one main shape with smaller shapes built round it, for example, "A fish against weeds". This gives plenty of scope for imagination and decorative treatment. All materials should be ironed carefully first of all so that there is no fear of puckering. The background material should be selected first. Any fabric such as linen or rayon which is firm will be suitable. The following suggestions for materials will give scope for the beginner, who can select the one nearest to her personal preference and to the concept of her design.

1   A dark greeny-blue background suggesting sea-water; bright pink cotton for the fish with a deeper red for the stripes; yellow organdie for the weeds.
2   Blue and white striped mattress ticking for the sea; orange felt for the fish with red sequins for the markings on it, and a button for the eye; green woollen material for the weed.
3   Any material with a small pattern that suggests sea-waves, for example, a dark blue background with white scrolls on it; a piece of red flannel for the fish with pink felt for the fins; green rayon with grey net placed on top of it for the weeds.

Iron all the pieces flat so that they are easier to work with. This applies to all fabrics for future use except velvet, which should never be ironed, but steamed over a kettle to take out all the creases.

In order to plan the design, choose from a reference book a fish which has an interesting shape and which lends itself to decorative purposes; or, better still, visit an aquarium where you can make some drawings of fish. Here are a few suggestions:

an angel fish	long-spined choetodon
perch	flying-fish
red fire fish	plaice

III *Henry VIII:* by Josephine Jordan

One of these can be copied in pencil, drawn with a pen in blue or Indian ink, or painted with a brush using Indian ink or water-colour. (First method.)

The main part can be cut out straight away in paper or material. (Second method.) People who would be frightened at the thought of *drawing* a design find it quite easy to make a simple shape with scissors as these tools which are so often employed for dressmaking and so on can be handled more naturally.

The main outline of the design can be traced from the book on to greaseproof or tracing paper. (Third method.)

Sometimes a drawing or tracing has to be enlarged. A ruler can be used but a set-square makes for greater accuracy. Using this draw round the design with measurements that can be divided into quarter inches. Draw lines a quarter inch apart over the picture from top to bottom and from left to right, dividing the whole into small sections, each a quarter inch square. Now draw out on white paper a similar rectangle with the same number of squares, making them 1 inch square instead of $\frac{1}{4}$ inch square. This enlarges the picture area four times. If you want the picture larger make the rectangle proportionately larger. Each section of the design can be re-drawn square by square. If there are a great many squares it is simpler to follow if they are numbered accordingly.

Now choose one or two weed shapes such as feathered seaweed or carrageen moss seaweed, or if it is difficult to find reference books adapt the shape of leaves like those from the box tree, the willow, rowan, oak, walnut, sycamore or yew. Look at the way they grow from the stem, either opposite each other or alternately. Even if you decide to pick one type of leaf for all your needs it can be made to look quite different according to the choice of stitches or material selected, so that the design can be built up elaborately or simply according to how adventurous the designer is feeling. Draw or cut the weed behind the fish making certain that good clear outlines are obtained with essentially simple shapes so that there is no final effect of a solid wedge and general overcrowding.

Place the background material on a firm surface, and using tacking stitches make a rectangle an inch smaller all round. This is to provide a lap-over for mounting later. If the weed and fish are not being cut out straight away freehand, trace them separately and carefully pin them on to the selected fabrics, making sure that the weave or grain goes in the same direction as the background material and that if net is used the pull is just right so that it is taut and does not pucker. Cut out, making sharp direct incisions to get clear lines and shapes. Place the weed in position on the background material and then the fish. At this stage a piece of weed may have to be added, taken away or moved up, down or sideways to make a more interesting design. The fish may look more exciting with part of the seaweed breaking away and placed in front of it, thus giving an illusion of putting the fish farther in the distance. Add the stripes to the body and then pin the whole design into position. If rubber solution is going to be used it is easier to make light pencil marks just under the top and bottom of the main weeds and to make light marks on the background and weeds to help with the placing of the fish and the stripes on top. These markings can be made so that they do not show at all. Use an orange stick when applying the rubber solution. This saves unnecessary mess and is easy to use. Those who wish to sew the pieces on are advised to tack lightly first of all, then to undersew in neat small stitches with matching cotton. Take the tacking threads out. At this stage you might like to cover any frayed edges either with herring-bone stitch in the same colour or else couching stitch using a contrast. On the other hand, the frayed edges can be left to suggest the feathery movement of the weed against sea-water. A lighter look is obtained if net is left undersewn without any outline, and pieces can be cut away to reveal the full colour of the weed behind. Any additional stitches can be added to emphasize the weed—some suggestions are detached chain stitch, fly stitch, or feather stitch. For the fish rosette chain stitch, chevron stitch or double back-stitch can be used. Sequins make decorative patterns, either attached with a small bead in the middle or stitched with threads going from the outside to the centre to form a star shape. The fins and tail can be made from additional material, couched or uneven Cretan stitch. Contrasts in the stitching can be made by using thick and thin threads; thin ones can be obtained by dividing a strand and using one or two pieces. For the eye, a bead, sequin or buttonhole stitch designed in the form of a circle can be used.

PRESSING AND MOUNTING

If beads and sequins have not been used, the finished work can be placed face downwards and carefully pressed with a warm iron over a damp cloth. The alternative, particularly where velvet has been used, because ironing disturbs the pile, is to stretch the picture in this way: place three thicknesses of damp blotting paper large enough to form a framework round the picture on to a flat surface, a board, an old wooden table or a wooden floor. Pin it in place firmly and lay the picture over it, the right side facing upwards. Starting from the centre of the top and bottom edges place the drawing pins about an inch apart and work in this way down the two sides, making certain that the work is flat and the right shape. Leave this to dry for at least a day, and do not remove it until it is no longer damp to the touch.

Cut the cardboard for mounting so that it is an inch smaller than the background material. Then turn back the edges of the fabric over the board using the tacking stitches as a guide, and either stick or sew them down firmly so that the picture is flat and taut. Linen thread is recommended, using one or two strands according to the weight of the material. Catch the middle of the picture from the top centre to the bottom centre. Repeat the stitching up and down towards each end; then from the left to the right centres on to the ends until the picture is secure. When fresh threads have to be used make sure the old ones have been well finished off. Neaten the corners by folding or mitring and then oversew them.

The picture is now ready for framing.

HOW TO MAKE A PICTURE—(B) BY MACHINE

(1) *Using felt*

Beginners may also like to try some machine embroidery. It is really only "drawing with a needle" instead of a pencil or brush. Used alone or combined with a little hand embroidery it can produce charming and sophisticated results. Apart from using a machine with special fittings for different types of stitches, variations can be made by

(i)   altering the number of stitches to the inch,

(ii) using one coloured cotton in the top reel and a different colour in the bobbin,

(iii) using braids, wools, etc., and attaching them with running stitches to the material. Some people may find it helpful to work with an embroidery hoop to keep the work firmer while others may prefer to work without and to have the fabric free.

"A fish and weeds" can also be used as a motif for a machine picture, although in this case it would be simpler and more decorative to have the fish against the background and a piece of weed placed each side of it. Felt is an ideal background, and a mottled pink and black, or mottled blue and black foundation would set a contemporary flavour. Vermilion felt could be used for the main shapes of the fish, pink cotton material for the oval decoration in the centre of the body, and yellow felt for the base of the eye. Green and black mottled felt on a bright yellow-green felt would be suitable for seaweed. Draw and cut out a typical fish shape, about $4\frac{1}{2}$ inches by $3\frac{1}{2}$, preferably with a broad body and not a narrow one. Either undersew or stick these pieces on. Cut out a fan-shaped piece of paper large enough to make a tail for the fish and pin this in position as a guide for the machining. Do a double line of running stitches round these edges, using pink cotton in both top reel and bobbin. Inside the fan-shaped tail make zig-zag lines for extra patterning. These can be quite haphazard, but if a neat repetition of lines is required the upper and lower points may be marked with a coloured pencil or a pin. When stitching, stop the machine at these points, with the needle in the material, then raise the presser foot and turn the fabric round in the new direction. Lower the presser foot and continue stitching. Using pale blue cotton and double stitching again follow the shape just inside the pink centrepiece on the fish. If you do not feel confident about tackling this on the actual fabric at once, practise on a piece of paper cut the same sort of shape, using the machine needle unthreaded. Next make the fins. Using red cottons make zig-zag lines from the machined blue outline to well away from the fish's body. Do this all round the fish, making the zig-zags smaller by the tail so that the tail patterning does not get muddled. Then between each zig-zag make blue lines to give variety. Finish off all ends by taking them through to the other side and knotting firmly. Yellow silk couched "feelers" may be added by hand, with French knots in the centre of the pink shape and on the tail. The eye can be buttonholed on with a French knot in the middle. Seaweed can be patterned with blue and yellow cotton French knots with pink star-shaped flowers for additional colour. Press the completed picture with a warm iron but do not use a damp cloth as this will stretch the felt. Mount the completed work as instructed in the hand-sewn fish.

(2) *Using net*

This is slightly more difficult but produces a fascinating quality. Why not be unconventional and choose a bright pink rayon background for a change?

Choose dark green net for the weed and while paying attention to the "pull" against the background material, cut it into a broad definite shape. Pin this to the fabric and double machine stitch with pale green cotton just within the edges (if taken too near the whole lot will fray and pull away). Choose green rayon for the fish and stick it well within the outer shape of the weed. On one half of the body pin a grey piece of net and on the other a piece of red, with the centre edge cut straight and the red overlapping the grey. Machine down the centre in red cotton. Finish off all ends. Threading up with black cotton, machine just within the outer shape of the body all round. Finish off. Then in white, machine round the outer edge of the body. Finish off. Cut away the rest of the net round the outside of the fish, carefully avoiding the machine stitches. A purple eye can be added in silk fabric covered with a small centre of black net. This may prove too small and finicky for a beginner to stitch by machine; if so, blanket stitch can be used and a French knot. The centre of the body could well have a smaller shape repeating the outer edges in white double machine stitch, and a variation on the zig-zag stitch used inside this with French knots to give additional interest. Remove any pins which might have been left in the fabric. Press carefully with a warm iron on the back of the design, and mount as instructed previously.

FRAMING

You may have been working to the size of an old frame which you already possess or which you have found in a junk shop, and you would like to change its colour. Sandpaper it down first of all, clean the surface with turpentine and paint with flat white and, if desired, a touch of oil colour. Art stores sell small sizes of student's colours or flat emulsion paint tinted with water colour. If the original frame was black or a dark brown a second coat may be required.

Alternatively the local woodwork store would make up a frame from a moulding and would mitre the corners. This could be painted if required.

Picture framers can often give helpful suggestions for framing if you are at all uncertain as to the type of frame which might suit the work or the room it is to occupy, or whether the picture may be too heavy for the moulding.

A mount round a picture often enhances it and glass is essential because this keeps the picture free from dust and discoloration. It is better to get the mount cut professionally at an art store for a small charge. Nothing looks so drab as a badly

IV *Queen Elizabeth I:* by Eugenie Alexander

cut board and it is a difficult process for the amateur. It can be off-white, grey or coloured to echo a tone in the picture or to contrast with it. It should, however, reflect the mood of the subject and not cancel it out or put it second in importance.

It may be helpful to note the types of frames used for some of the pictures illustrating this book.

"Hermon Chapel" (Plate 32) has a linen "box" frame with a gold edge.

"Tea by the River" (Plate 2) has a magenta mount with black net stretched over it and a white frame with a single moulding.

"Queen Elizabeth I" (Plate IV) has a green velvet "box" frame, which allows for the padded quality and does not squash the materials against the glass.

"The Dragonfly" (Plate 45) has a red mount with a limed and waxed oak frame.

"Henry VIII" (Plate III) has a frame usually sold for oil-paintings with a gold line inside the outer moulding.

"Abstract No. 4" (Plate 9) has a narrow white frame treated with gesso.

GENERAL HINTS AND REMINDERS

Sorting rag-bag pieces

1. Save all the odd remnants of materials that appeal to you. There are various ways of sorting them so that they will be easier to select when you require them for pictures.

(*a*) Keep silks, organdies, felts and so on in separate bundles.

(*b*) Keep patterned pieces apart from plain ones.

(*c*) Keep warm colours like reds, yellows and oranges in a separate pile from the cold colours, grey, green and blue.

Keep these materials in paper bags or boxes, labelled for easy reference and preferably ironed to make them more inviting. Polythene bags are slightly more expensive, but as one can see at once what is in them, they save the trouble of labelling.

Ideas

2. Keep a box or a loose-leaf scrapbook for cuttings from magazines, newspapers and for sketches of ideas for pictures.

3. When making use of natural forms (e.g. flowers) look at the patterning of their growth, and the formation and placing of leaves and petals. Get to know what are the essentials to leave in and what can be left out.

Look around you and at nature with a view to translating it into shapes and patterns for fabrics and stitches. Note the silhouettes of objects which will act as a rough guide to the shape.

Other things besides books, magazines, films and television can suggest ideas. Music lovers can often conjure up pictures in their minds of certain music, like "Carnival of the Animals" by Saint-Saens and Prokofiev's "Peter and the Wolf". Stories and poems will lead to this mind picture-making, too. "The Prodigal Son" is full of possibilities and one could make a design incorporating the whole parable either in rectangles or naturally leading from one scene to the next with grape-vines making a decorative pattern round each incident.

4. It is a mistake to try and be too realistic. Let the texture of the fabric and the type of stitches used create the suggestion of a tree or butterfly that could only come from this medium. The simplest shapes of a leaf or a wing can look individual and interesting if the material is well chosen and the stitches suitably placed so that they echo and enhance the design.

5. Realize that scissors are your working tool and that this will give certain limitations, such as ruling out excessive detail in cutting. Exploit the potentialities of the medium and have respect for the limitations. These are the short cuts to success.

6. To begin with choose a subject with an obvious shape and a clean outline, which is simple to cut out and is also something that has a distinct leaning towards flat patterning, as a "3D" or solid effect is difficult to achieve. For instance, an early Egyptian head from a bas-relief with its emphasis on flat, two-dimensional appearance is more fitting than trying to express the solidity of a realistic Greek head in sculpture. Later more elaborate ideas can be tried but it is more rewarding to achieve something pleasing at the start and not become disappointed because too much has been demanded without the practice required.

Designing the Picture

7. Good and easily workable sizes for pictures range from 5 by 7 inches to approximately 40 by 30 inches. If the size is smaller than 5 by 7 it can be difficult and tedious to work on but if it is a good deal larger than 30 by 25 it can be difficult to handle and it also tends to become a wall-hanging instead of a picture.

8. When designing with several shapes choose one main object but do not put it in the dead centre of the picture as this can give too symmetrical an appearance. If smaller shapes or ideas are arranged round the main motif a more interesting balance can be achieved.

9. Do not cram your picture with shapes so that the eye travels chaotically over the surface and has no resting place or main interest. Simpler designs are sometimes more fitting for contemporary rooms.

10. A picture may be in the form of:
(*a*) a vignette,
(*b*) an "all over" design more like a painting,
(*c*) a decorative, flat patterned design,
(*d*) a three-dimensional and more solid design.

11. Ideas for designs may be:
(*a*) traced from a drawing, then cut out in fabric,
(*b*) cut out straight away from paper, juggled with, arranged on a board, then traced from this arrangement and cut out in fabric from the tracings,

(*c*) drawn straight away lightly in pencil on to fabric and cut out,

(*d*) cut out freehand in cartridge paper, attached to the fabric and cut again,

(*e*) cut out straight away from the fabric.

Choice of Background Materials

12. Don't be afraid to try coloured backgrounds. Pale linen was used years ago only because there were no alternatives. Choose material that is strong, firm and not easily pulled out of shape. Cut it so that it is 1 inch larger than the drawn design in order to have a generous overlap when the mounting has to be done. Mark this out with tacking stitches as a guide.

13. When choosing materials place them roughly in position against the background fabric to see if the colours harmonize before attempting to set about the cutting out. Sometimes a colour seems suitable in its original bulk but when it is reduced to the shape required it is either too strong in colour or tone for the other shapes or not strong enough. This can only be overcome by trial and error and experience.

Colour

14. It will be found that the colour of a fabric will vary according to whether it is lying flat for instance on the floor, or hanging on a wall. A difference may also be noticed according to whether the main source of light is coming from the left or from the right.

15. Do not use too many colours in your picture. In a strange way the use of too many colours leads to an impression of "no colour at all", whereas a few used wisely will give a rich and lovely effect of colour.

16. Work for good contrasts of colour combined with harmony.

17. Remember to use colours to create depth and intensity. Don't pick the first red that comes to hand from your rag-bag, for indeed a crimson fabric can be light, medium or dark in tone. If you choose two crimsons and two greens which are all light in tone there will be no real contrast or interest even though they *are* contrasting colours. To find out more about tone look at fabrics and at your surroundings with half-closed eyes. This provides a guide to tone relationship. If you hold your background complete with pinned pieces up to a mirror this will also give you a new viewpoint and help towards any required alterations.

18. To achieve a gay picture use mainly bright warm colours against a few sombre shades to prevent gaudiness. To achieve a more solemn effect more subdued, colder colours should be used.

19. Try making a picture using white fabric only. You will be surprised at the variety of colour, tone and texture you can achieve. Use white threads with black, grey, gold or silver threads for a contrast.

20. A picture of greys, or black and white, can look very sophisticated. Choose suitable subjects.

Texture

21. It may also be found that, depending on the distribution and size of various shapes, some heavy materials (velvet, felt) may not look right with some light-textured materials (organza). The "weight" may be over-emphasized in the wrong places and a true "marriage" of materials is not achieved. This is something that comes with more practice and more knowledge of texture.

Ironing Materials

22. Iron flat all pieces except velvet before making the picture. This is essential. They not only look more inviting but are easier to work with. Do not iron velvet but boil a kettle of water and steam it over the spout.

Tracing

23. When a tracing is made from a pencil design it is helpful to mark horizontal and vertical lines on each traced shape so that they will correspond with the warp and weft of the background material.

Pinning and Placing

24. When pinning pieces on make certain that the grain of the fabric corresponds with the grain of the background. If this is not done the pieces will buckle after a short time.

25. Even when a previous drawing has been made, pin *all* pieces of material on to the background material before starting, making certain that the work is on a flat surface such as a board or table. The pieces may have to be juggled around or they may not be in suitable positions when the final selection of materials has been made. Some things may have to be left out and others put in. In order to allow for these adjustments a border (larger than the 1 inch left all round for mounting) may be advisable for beginners, so that the shapes of the design will not be too close to the edges and be lost behind the framing at the finish.

26. Make shapes show up against other shapes by:

(*a*) using a warm colour (orange, red, yellow) against a cool colour (grey, green, blue),

(*b*) a patterned texture against a plain one,

(*c*) a light colour next to a dark colour,

(*d*) a shiny thread near one with a matt quality.

27. To give the illusion of distance:

(*a*) use warm colours for shapes in the front of the picture and cool colours for the shapes at the back to make them recede.

(*b*) place large figures or objects in the front of the picture and small figures or objects at the back.

When more confidence has been achieved start overlapping objects for added interest. When cutting shapes for these trace out or draw out straight away the whole of the under shape on to the material. There will then be no awkward gap from wrong parts cut away when another shape is laid on top.

Attaching Fabric Pieces to Background Material

28. When a shape, for example an arm made from silk, overlaps, say, a body made from a thick material like felt, it is sometimes best to cut out and include the smaller felt shape of the arm joined to the body and then stick the silk over it so that no bump is left.

29. Pieces of fabric may be attached to the background material by:

(*a*) undersewing,

(*b*) sticking with rubber solution,

(*c*) machine stitching (plain stitch or zig-zag stitch),

(*d*) using a stout nylon thread and catching the materials firmly in the appropriate places. See that they are placed in the right order.

30. When rubber solution is used for a picture and one shape overlaps another, make a small pencil mark where it will not show as guidance for placing.

31. When using rubber solution do not use too much as this can spoil light textured materials and is unnecessarily messy.

Raw Edges

32. Raw edges may be:

(*a*) left frayed, thus using a natural effect of the fabric,

(*b*) stuck together by running an orange stick with rubber solution on it along the frayed part,

(*c*) couched,

(*d*) camouflaged by using herring-bone stitch,

(*e*) machined with one of the decorative machine stitches such as a zig-zag effect which can be achieved on several machines.

Stitching (by hand)

33. Don't make your picture an example of all the different stitches you can cram together. This spoils the final effect by confusion. A few used well give a unity. Vary the thickness of thread used. Stranded cotton has six strands. Use two, three or one for variation.

34. If any new stitches are attempted, try them out first on a separate piece of material until a natural rhythm is established and the stitches can be executed unselfconsciously.

35. Use short lengths of thread. This will avoid unnecessary tangles.

36. Contours of shapes can be emphasized by a line of couched stitching not only on the outside of the fabric, but just inside it.

37. Do not try to pull thread through the eye of a needle which is too small for it. This will not only eventually break the needle but make a hole in the background material and the fabric shape itself.

6 *Owl and House:* by Christine Risley

7 *Woman and Birds:* by Christine Risley
(*Property of Nottinghamshire Education Committee*)

38. Avoid long threads leading from, say, a shape on the left hand side of the picture to another on the right. This will lead to puckering and, like knots, has an irritating way of showing through certain materials. So finish off and start again.

39. Make certain that the stitches used are for a definite purpose and form an interesting pattern in themselves. When stitches are used in too haphazard a way a muddle can ensue.

40. Practise starting off by making small running stitches and then working back on these, on the back of the background material, instead of knotting the thread. Sometimes a knot shows through the material and lends anything but interest! When finishing off, take the needle through to the back of the background material and slip it firmly through some of the stitches. Cut the thread.

Stitching (by machine)

41. The various sewing machines on the market differ in instructions for embroidery stitching. Read the booklet for your own type thoroughly before starting.

42. It is advisable not to use the machine for designing after a tiring day because although when one is used to it it has a fascinating flexibility, it does not respond to the amateur like the needle in hand embroidery, when the hand movements often have a relaxing effect. The machine does need more concentration and a fresh mind, otherwise it can seem to become a terrifying monster likely to run away with one! Besides this, machine stitches need more patience in the unpicking if there are many interlacing lines.

43. Each machine has its own personality which the owner will gradually recognize as they co-operate together.

44. For easier and happier working make certain that the table is the right height. In order to gain better control over speed on electric machines place the foot controller as far away as possible as this will make the leg more relaxed.

45. Advice can be sought from machine manufacturers. At Singer sewing centres used machines can be hired for 2s. 6d. an hour and work can be done on the spot.

Hand models

46. A hand model naturally leaves only one hand free for the embroidery unless one has a careful assistant, but it is surprising how one can manage to achieve an effective design in simple running stitches if the wheel is turned in rhythm with one's capacity to guide the left hand for this purpose.

47. When any intricate moving of the material has to be done, stop the machine and use both hands to manipulate the fabric into the required position. This will eliminate the possibility of forcing against the needle.

48. Avoid tight curves and small circles. These will buckle the material and

probably break the needle as it is only the machine that is set up for advanced machine embroidery that can tackle this problem efficiently.

49. The presser-foot is a helpful aid for following a lightly pencilled outline.

Electric and treadle machines

50. In order to leave both hands free for simple machine embroidery, it is necessary to have a treadle or electrically driven domestic sewing machine. The presser foot is removed so that the stitching and design can be seen more clearly, and the teeth-feed retracted or masked. Instead of straight lines, free stitching can then be attempted, e.g. circles, curves and satin stitch. Adjust the stitch marker to a smaller sized stitch and thread up the machine in the usual way. You can either place the part of your picture that you wish to start on into a round tambour frame, stretching it so that it is taut, or leave the material free. Set it in position with the needle at a convenient part of the design. Depress the presser foot lever and begin work, using both hands to manipulate the frame backwards, forwards, in circles, or side to side. By guiding the material in the frame quickly and making the machine run slowly long stitches appear, slow movement of the frame gives short stitches. When the work is finished cut off the beginning and end threads close to the work.

51. Electric motors can be fitted on to most hand models.

52. Some machines have discs and levers for zig-zag stitching. For machines which have not got these, a zig-zag attachment can be purchased. This can be fitted on to most machines, including hand models, but care must be taken not to move the material in jerks if a regular pattern is required.

53. On a simple domestic machine variations of stitch length, fine and heavy threads, and colour variations, such as a red cotton in the top reel with blue cotton in the bobbin, can produce interesting effects. For the more adventurous or able handed, braid, ribbon and wool can be machined on to fabric shapes. A cable-stitch, which produces a thick cable-like effect, can be tried by using thicker threads such as pearl cotton or fine metal thread wound round the spool with mercerized sewing-cotton in the needle. This has to be worked on the wrong side of the material, using tacking stitches (making sure that they show through from the right side) as a guide to the design required. Two or three lines close together can look very effective. Multiple lines of black stitching can separate areas of brilliant colour so that they will appear to be in a jewel-like setting. A raised effect makes a contrast. This also has to be done on the wrong side using the quilting foot with the little steel bar pulled out. (This acts as a guide for straight quilting only.)

Electric machines which produce embroidery stitches automatically

54. These are designed for people who like to see the finished stitches appear before their very eyes instead of having to make up their own stitches. The latest models will machine forwards and backwards and will work a variety of embroidery stitches automatically by flicking levers or by disc selection.

55. By adjustment of width of stitch, stitch position and length of stitch, different effects can be achieved.

56. Try out stitches on a scrap of material and see if they fit the purpose for which they are intended. Sometimes a double line of stitching, use of a twin needle, or reverse line of stitching can be added for extra richness and strength.

57. The wider zig-zag stitch is a favourite for raw edge camouflage because it seems to unite the shape and the background instead of divorcing one from the other as often happens when a close, heavy stitch is used.

General hints for all types of machine

58. Always make sure that the lever is in the highest possible position before starting and finishing work.

59. Keep material flat to avoid buckling.

60. Tangles sometimes result because the threads have not been pulled out properly behind. The machine will jam if it is allowed to run when the material has been placed so that the needle just misses it, or if the cottons have been cut too short after threading up.

61. Wrong tensions, thickness of cotton and size of needles used can cause puckering and faulty stitching.

62. When using Lurex non-tarnishing metallic yarn (metallized Mylar) keep the tension very light. When used in the reel keep it straight and choose the correct needle. In some machines fancy stitching with Lurex is more attractive when used in the bobbin only, but flat and even winding must be maintained. With care it can be used for top and bottom threads. Speed should be reduced to one-half to one-third less than normal.

63. Avoid vulgarity by limiting stitch designs if you have a machine which produces several varieties automatically. Whatever the type of machine it is interesting to mix hand embroidery stitching with machine stitching to avoid sameness of style. The delicacy of the fine pen-like machine stitching contrasts with the heavier style of the hand embroidered stitching.

64. Finishing off varies with different machines. In some the threads have to be knotted by hand. In others threads can be cut close to the material or are secured by making a few stitches without moving the work, or by running stitches backwards.

65. When unpicking has to be done it is a quicker and simpler job to cut the pieces slowly and carefully with sharp scissors and to make certain all the bits of thread have been removed. It is most irritating to find little bobbles creeping under the applied pieces. Or a "Quickunpic" gadget is useful for machine stitches.

Ironing and Stretching

66. If an iron is used to press a picture flat instead of the stretching process, make sure no velvet or sequins have been used. The pile of the velvet will be spoilt and the sequins will melt.

67. When damp blotting paper is used for stretching, make sure the picture is dry before it is unpinned.

Mounting

If by any chance the design has been so changed that there is not enough background material left to turn over the mounting board, either machine or stick on some matching or suitably contrasting material. If it will not show but is just required for a lap-over use a piece of binding securely hemmed or machined.

68. Do not use brown cardboard for mounting. The chemical content in it may eventually destroy the colours in the materials.

69. When mounting a picture make sure the threads used are strong and are pulled tight, and that the non-staining rubber solution or glue used has a strong holding power.

CHAPTER III

Ideas for Pictures

1 IDEAS SUGGESTED BY FABRIC TEXTURES

THE textures of pieces of fabric in themselves often suggest a subject for a picture. For example:

A blue and white cotton material with scrolled pattern on it . . . sea waves.

A piece of woollen material with a multi-coloured design based on various sized overlapping circles . . . a crowd or pieces of rock on a beach.

A piece of grey flannel from an old shirt . . . an elephant.

Black and yellow striped lamé . . . a tiger.

A piece of green soft suède . . . a rubbery hot-house plant.

Grey chiffon and white net . . . fleecy clouds.

Black open-work lace . . . wrought iron railings.

Budgerigar's cast-off feathers, especially the tail ones . . . a feather for a hat, or part of a bird's tail.

A snippet of gaily coloured silk cut from a blouse which you are making, lying curled up on the floor can suggest a fantastic flower.

Red and white striped cotton . . . an umbrella for a café scene.

Pale grey velvet . . . a Siamese cat.

Beads and buttons . . . eyes.

Pearls and sequins . . . a clown for the nursery.

Small shells . . . an under-water scene.

Look at odd scraps and amuse yourself by trying to conjure up how you would use them. There are endless possibilities!

2 IDEAS SUGGESTED BY THE USE OF STITCHES

Now try and go further by selecting pieces and imagining what is required in the way of stitch embellishment to transform them into the required subject. For instance:

(i) a spotted yellow and white material with a red fly stitch going in the same direction at the base of some of the spots will enliven the effect and suggest the texture of a bird's body, while feather stitches on strips of blue silk suggest a tail.

(ii) Cretan stitches at the top of a green piece of silk will suggest a bird's wing-tips.

(iii) A piece of coffee-coloured linen with herring-bone stitch used on it will make a summer hat; alternatively chain stitching would suggest plaited straw.

43

(iv) A piece of coral-red felt with lines of blanket stitch which are placed down so that the vertical lines start in the centres of the preceding row of horizontal lines will give the effect of tile-work.

(v) A piece of dark grey tweed with pale grey wool bullion knots can portray a sheep's curly coat.

(vi) Silver lamé with pale grey nylon thread and white silk Cretan stitches imaginatively arranged can give the effect of a shining star.

(vii) Crimson velvet with fine green cotton detached chain stitch can give the effect of strawberry markings.

(viii) Several brilliant colours cut into shapes and couched with black wool will give the impression of a stained glass window with its black leadings.

(ix) Wools, silks and raffia can be transformed into hair if they are couched into a natural hair line or chain-stitched or made into French knots.

On looking at the diagrams of embroidery stitches produced automatically by various makes of sewing machine, the following ideas come to mind:

(*a*) one which would give an effect of bricks,

(*b*) a representation of massed leaves,

(*c*) decorative railings,

(*d*) a pattern on a woollen jumper,

(*e*) a flight of steps,

(*f*) little trees (as seen from a distance),

(*g*) sea waves,

(*h*) pebbles on a beach,

(*i*) a line of bottles on a shelf.

Readers might enjoy trying to guess which ones I chose and also making up new ideas for themselves.

With practice the beginner can soon sense the right sort of stitch which will further express a feeling for the texture of the object the fabric is creating.

3 SUGGESTIONS FOR REFERENCE

(a) From Museums and Churches

Not everyone feels confident enough to make things up out of their head straight away without a little inspiration. The following ideas may help towards the day when imagination, design and colour come without these stimuli, but pictures with an original flavour can be made with the help of these ideas if the materials chosen are interesting and colourful. It is often helpful to select and adapt ideas which have already been simplified for certain media such as:

(i) Staffordshire pottery figures which can be seen in antique shops and museums. Brighton Art Gallery have a fascinating and varied collection. A china dog or lady on horseback could be carried out in pink silk and white felt.

(ii) The 17th-century stump work pictures which can be seen in antique shops and in various musuems (the Victoria and Albert Museum and Brighton Art

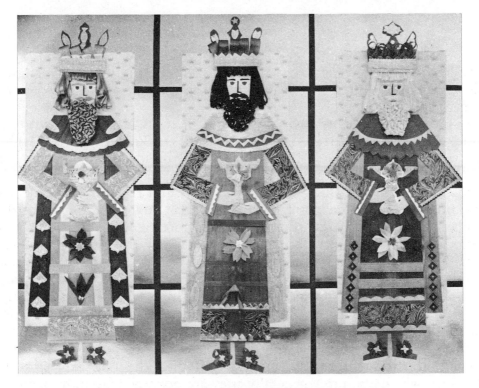

8 *The Three Kings:* by Eugenie Alexander
(*Property of Hallmark*)

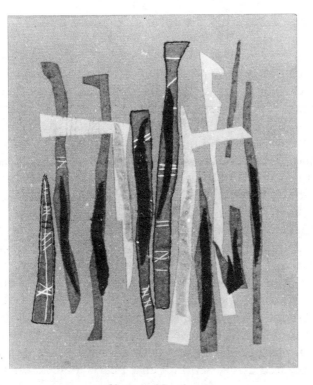

9 *Abstract Number 4:*
by Eugenie Alexander

Gallery for instance) give a variety of ideas incorporating people, animals, birds and flowers. "Queen Elizabeth I" (Plate IV) is an example of stump work brought up to date.

Dora Owen, aged eighty-two, makes silk pictures with an electric sewing machine which she has such an affection for she has nicknamed it Dorcas after the woman mentioned in the New Testament. She introduces a 20th-century version of the 18th-century silk pictures (mentioned in Chapter I). Her favourite subjects are landscapes (many of which stand out in parts and give the illusion of a third dimension) often based on postcard reproductions and portraits enlarged from newspaper cuttings. A very realistic embroidered portrait of Sir Winston Churchill, with special attention paid to bringing out the qualities of his personality—his intellect, humour and pugnacity—hangs in the Speaker's House. She has had art and machine-embroidery lessons and prefers the fabric and machine medium because of the effects of light which she can get in the eyes, the rough appearance of hair and the subtle modelling and colouring which is achieved by a choice of over one hundred and forty fine art silks and by variations of speed, silk and tension on spool and reel. She makes a drawing, traces it on to organdies, backs this with casement cloth and fits it into an embroidery frame. The long satin stitches and small circles which she most generally uses are governed by movement of the frame between her hands. She has exhibited in the Enfield Art Exhibition and reproductions of her pictures have appeared in English, Australian and Canadian papers.

(iii) Brass rubbings from churches form interesting motifs.

(b) Prints

(i) Redouté flower prints present small sprays of flowers for reference which are placed in happy relation to their plain background. From these, and better still from nature direct, study the general direction and pattern of growth and evolve a style which suggests the general feeling, shape and texture of a flower but does not seek to copy nature too closely. This will produce lively results. Look at the proportions of the spaces left round the flowers, buds and leaves and perhaps choose coloured backgrounds. Plants can be worked in fine nets and chiffons with machine embroidery, in heavier materials with hand embroidery or in a contrasting mixture of both these methods.

(ii) Victorian engraved prints from antique shops. Theodosia Townshend is a contemporary exponent of tinsel and fabric pictures. These began when she made a drawing of her two dachshunds and decided to put them in a "bed" of real material. So many of her friends admired them that she was encouraged to make more works of this kind. She never repeats her designs and uses old lithographs and engravings of landscapes, Napoleon, the Empress Eugenie, and the ballet. A small picture showing the ballerina Louise Taglioni against a grey and white painted background, red silk gathered curtains with additional braid, a pink chiffon ballet skirt with white pleated frills, sequins and pearls placed on top, was especially

10 *Madonna and Child:* by John Noble

charming. Pearls were also round her neck, wrist and silk bodice. The wings were from the original engraving, also her head, arms and legs.

Another delightful picture was "The shell grotto at Windsor". The only fabric here was the little girl's dress of white gathered chiffon with red ribbon and red velvet shoes. Shells decorated the edges and there was a scalloped effect at the top. Tiny pebbles were stuck on the ground and the wall in front of the engraved castle was made of layers of crumbly soft sandstone.

(c) Public Libraries

These have books with excellent reproductions which help with design, colour and subject matter. The following ideas can be referred to:

(i) The mosaics of Ravenna. A picture with the rich head-dresses of the Empress Theodora and her Court made in pieces of coloured felt and jewels on a black ground would be stimulating, effective and interesting.

(ii) Certain pictures by the metaphysical painter Paul Klee such as "Sun and Moon flowers" which has a dream-like, lyrical and abstract quality. An original picture could be adapted using some of these shapes with nylon threads, organdies and dupions laid on top of each other.

(iii) Marc Chagall's poetic pictorial images serve to remind us that no holds are barred in picture making. In "Cow with parasol" he has used various images in one picture; such improbabilities as a white cow with a blue face holding a parasol, a hand on its back holding a bouquet; a calf, a rooster, yellow roof tops, a large orange and yellow sun become a wonderful world of make believe, yet are freely adapted from the world in which he lives.

(iv) The Bayeux Tapestry with its simple method of telling a historical story may give ideas for making a domestic record of your own family as they grow up and go out to school and to work. For those who do dressmaking it would amuse younger members of the family if left-over pieces of material were used for their frocks in miniature.

(v) The simple bold lines which Byzantine artists used for their work are a guide to the beginner. An adaption of the Madonna and Child in Duccio di Buoninsegna's "The Madonna and Child with Saints" would make a striking fabric picture. The tilt of the Madonna's head, the placing of the hands, the small child (the exaggeration of the smallness of the child in comparison with the adult figure was used symbolically in those days to draw more attention to the Christ Child) are all interesting features. A Russian icon has been adapted by John Noble in "The Madonna and Child" (Plate 10). Another religious picture, "The Annunciation" by Simone Martini, has a very beautiful stylized angel kneeling with flowers in the hair and a lovely pattern of leaves held in the hands. The enormous patterned wings offer possibilities for decoration using beads, pearls, lace and stitching.

(vi) Dutch paintings of flower pieces which use various mixtures and shapes in one picture such as a hyacinth, narcissus, lily, tulip, rose, ferns, butterflies and even birds' nests with eggs. Jacobius van Heuysium painted several examples using baskets as well as vases for the flowers to stand in. Different backgrounds can be used, a window with gauze showing the sky through it perhaps, or a rich velvet curtain, but keep it simple in design as too much pattern will cancel out the colour and texture of the flowers.

(vii) A more formal stylized version can be seen in a French 17th-century embroidered panel. The one I have in mind is in yellow-brown velvet applied to blue cloth with heavy couching. A finer gold thread might be substituted for this and a yellow woollen background used with luscious crimson velvets for some of the flowers with dark green velvet leaves. Alternatively a raised effect could be acquired by cutting pieces of felt a shade smaller than the materials chosen for the flowers and case, and placed neatly underneath them.

(viii) As I mentioned in Chapter I, Jean Lurçat's tapestry designs are very stimulating, not only in rich colour contrasts but in treatment of shape and texture.

(ix) Thomas Bewick's engravings reveal a wonderful variety of texture in his pictures of birds and animals. A close study of wings and tail feathers will help with ideas for the type of stitches to use, but do not be tempted to overcrowd or completely fill the shapes. Subtle suggestion with patterned stitching in one or two places so that the material plays its part will make a far more pleasing picture.

(x) Nicholas Hilliard's portrait miniature of a young Elizabethan nobleman is attractive because of the thorny wild roses which are painted so that they form a pattern against the simple background of the cloak, hose and ruff.

(d) Postcard Reproductions

The following postcard reproductions can be purchased from museums, art stores and stationers and a selection might be useful. For example:

(i) Still Life Groups
  (a) Cézanne's "Onions and bottle" illustrates the wonderful impression of colour which can be achieved with subtle tones of pinks and greys. The solid semi-rounded shapes of the onions contrast with the fine rambling lines of the sprouting leaves.
  (b) Vincent van Gogh's "The breakfast table" shows an interesting group of a flower-patterned cup and jug, a blue and white checked jug, an interestingly shaped coffee pot with a thin handle, and the play of yellow background against a blue cloth. The smaller shapes of apples and lemons lend vitality.
  (c) Georges Braque's flat-patterned apples and leaves on a white plate and a glass on a white cloth against a green textured background show how by using simple shapes and playing with contrasting white and greens, a striking and beautiful picture results. The glass here has a counter-change treatment; half is in shadow, half is in the light.

(ii) Landscape

(*a*) Graham Sutherland's "Entrance to a lane" in yellow, green and dark browns presents nature in a form which gives rise on looking at this mystical transcription to the proposition that "a landscape is a feeling".

(*b*) Picasso's "Mediterranean landscape" is full of suggestions for original treatment of a holiday scene. The triangular use of shape, the bright colour and the patterning are food for thought.

(*c*) Henri Rousseau's "Virgin forest" shows a variety of foliage in soft greens, yellow and pink flowers, and huge tropical plants with a hot red sun.

(*d*) Pieter Brueghel's "Winter" with the large figure looming in the foreground and the scenery in the distance is helpful in obtaining perspective in later works. The greens, browns and whites convey in feeling and colour the essence of the season.

(iii) Portraits

(*a*) Georges Rouault's "The old king" is a fine and striking picture. It might be interesting to experiment with large blocks of colour against outlines of black velvet and use some rich jewels and pearls.

(*b*) A background of butterflies, flowers and foliage forms an attractive patterned surface for the plainer head-dress and clothes of the Princess in Pisanello's "Portrait of a Princess".

(iv) Animals

"A game of Polo", a 16th-century Persian illumination, has stylized horses with round chubby bodies and thin elegant legs and faces. The decorative and detailed pattern qualities of Persian work (trees, plants, birds and so on) are well worth contemplation.

(*e*) Commercial Art

Posters can often help with inspiration. One that I have in mind issued by London Transport showed a wonderful approach towards design by Betty Swanwick. This was a "Wedding" with the bride and bridegroom in front of the church porch. Behind them were the guests and in front six bridesmaids, with enormous bouquets, and five cats which appeared to be dancing. The pattern of the cats' legs and the placing of the bridesmaids and the other shapes in the picture are well worth some study.

(*f*) Ideas from Photographs reproduced in Newspapers

Often these contain unusual compositions seen from new angles.

(i) An abstract picture could be made from contrasting shapes derived from the twisted patterns of geranium seeds in flight, part of the skin of a sole, magnified 70 times, or the scales of silver fish magnified 170 times.

(ii) The patterning of a street with Chinese shops in the distance and just the heads and shoulders of figures in the foreground, seen by night.

(iii) The light from a fire and fireworks exploding in the sky, the rest of the picture being dark with the echoing dark silhouetted figures of children on Guy Fawkes night.

(iv) A scene of cliffs, sea and small rocks vignetted in bright light against the interior of a dark cave with a man standing looking out by the entrance.

(g) Ideas from Magazines

The following ideas are gleaned from cuttings from women's magazines and are an interesting collection which my mother (a keen amateur embroideress) made to keep by her for future adaption.

(i) An illustration of a farmyard scene; an angry farmer with hens and cocks scuttling round the yard and a black poodle in hot pursuit. A cockerel is perched high on a fence, a blackbird is flying from a tree and a gentle pig is leaning over a wall.

(ii) Or an illustration with a distinctly flat pattern quality which is particularly suitable for fabric pictures. Four people are seated round a table which has a hat, toy giraffe, rose, fruit and a boot on a cloth on the top. (This formed part of a guessing competition, if readers are wondering!)

(iii) An advertisement for soap of harlequin fish swimming against a background of rock and weeds.

(iv) Two reproductions of prints of the 1860 Exhibition at the Crystal Palace:
(a) The Hardware Gallery, with a galaxy of ornate bedsteads, pianos, chandeliers, flags and Victorian figures.
(b) Exhibits from India, with a stuffed elephant with a magnificent howdah, Indian attendants in richly coloured costumes, ornately looped curtains and patterned galleries.

(v) A Hungarian cushion design of stylized flowers and leaves based on traditional embroidery in the original colours, laurel green, gorse yellow, geranium and white, described as "the vivid colours of a summer day."

(vi) A plant painting reproduced from Curtis' *Botanical Magazine*, of "the Greater Bluebottle".

(vii) A coloured photograph of a black tailor's dummy wearing a pearl necklace and swathed with gaily coloured materials placed against a marble background with oranges, lemons and red roses.

All these pictures convey the sense of colour, texture, rhythm and design which is required for composing pictures.

CHAPTER IV

Artists and their Work

I HAVE written some biographies about some of the artists who make fabric pictures, several of whom have had one-man exhibitions, while most of the others have had work in mixed shows. While it is interesting to note the technique in pictures, it should be emphasized that it is the ideas behind them that count primarily. No amount of technical ability will make up for badly conceived designs which are mechanical and lacking in life, shape and originality. However, just as the creamy lushness of the paint itself plays a great part in one's enjoyment of a painting, so materials produce a sensation of their own in texture, pattern, colour and design. The following chapter deals with the personal ways in which selected artists use them to convey these sensations. It is unfortunately impossible to include all the artists who work in a fabric medium but I have taken a cross-section and used their pictures to illustrate certain points.

Perhaps, as a matter of convenience, I may be allowed to begin with an account of my own work.

From an early age, I am told, I showed a feeling for texture and colour. This was first observed by my parents, who one day thinking that their little daughter was being unnaturally quiet discovered that she was happily engrossed in spreading the dining-room wallpaper with a design made from the contents of a large pot of marmalade mixed with the dye from the poppies off her mother's favourite hat. In spite of this, my early artistic efforts in more orthodox media were widely encouraged. When I was 11 years old I went to a convent where I loved the art lessons and disliked doing dress-making and embroidery. Afterwards, at Chelsea School of Art, I studied book illustration for two years with Graham Sutherland, and had my first modelling tools made for me by Henry Moore. After the war I returned to Chelsea School of Art for four years and during this time while attaining my intermediate examination and the National Diploma in Design in Illustration, I was also trying my hand at various crafts such as lithography, fabric design and wood engraving, and doing some modelling and painting. In fact, I can see now, I was searching for a medium which appealed to me. Although one knows that technique as such can sometimes be taken too far, it is no use handling a pencil or a brush unless one finds them sympathetic to oneself and appropriate to the end in view. After further experiments with pottery and etching, the possibility of fabrics as a medium presented itself to me and my former dislike of doing embroidery vanished. Now "drawing" feather stitch with a needle and silk became a bird's tail, blanket stitch was a roof top. Here I found plenty of scope with the colour I loved, the kind

of texture I had been seeking. The flat pattern and decorative qualities which I enjoyed could both be suitably used in this style of picture making and a sewing machine could lend a quality of "drawing" somewhat akin to working with an etching needle.

"The Park" (Plate II) was made shortly after my husband and I had designed four window displays with figures in Elizabethan, Regency, Edwardian and present-day costumes made entirely of fabrics against green canvas backgrounds representing grass. The pieces of silk and rayon used for this picture were stuck on. "The Jays" (Plate 46) were entirely stitched, as invisibly as possible, and were studied from life. All the feathers were made up of layer upon layer of different coloured nets—silk materials were used for added glitter and felts for contrast texture. Among the colours were oranges, yellows, greens and beiges on a deep blue background.

"Europa and the Bull" (Plate 1) was a theme suggested by my husband who had just completed a painting of the same subject. At one time we had three widely different versions of this hanging round the room, the third one being made in petit-point by John Noble. There is a lot of white in my picture—a white bull, swans and other birds—all in felt. Europa wears a bright orange robe and the other maidens are in purple, cherry red and lemon yellow silks. The hair has been couched in various coloured silks while net and organdie have been used to achieve a misty effect on the mountain, the trees in the distance, birds' wings and tree trunk.

"Tea by the River" (Plate 2), came from a song from *Miss Hook of Holland* called "Come along with me to the Zoo, dear", which a friend of mine from Chelsea Art School used to sing. It was about a small girl being taken to tea with lions and tigers surrounding her. My version ended up as tea by the river. A mottled green felt was used for the grass and black net was placed over the top part to give distance. The lion was made from yellow ochre felt, with net for the modelled effects. I had some pink spotted cotton which had just the right-sized pattern for the little girl's dress. The man's jacket was blue and white checked cotton, again in just the right scale. The lion's mane was couched. French knots were used for the human eyes.

"Mountain Flowers" (Plate VI) is in nets, organdies, and rayons with pieces of lace for the cow parsley, sequins, beads and padded-in sections with felt placed under the silk.

"The Three Kings" commissioned by Hallmark was made out of their wrapping papers and ribbons. The sheen on the latter gave a stained-glass effect. Beards were made of knotted ribbon, and flowers, hair and crown were gathered to give a three-dimensional appearance.

"Abstract Number 4" is one of a series of pictures which I made when my 3-year-old son, John, had reached the stage of "helping" me—although he had grasped the essential ideas of picture-making (picking up snippets of gold lamé and saying "little butterfly" or glittering silver left-over leaf shapes which were "fishes"), these didn't look so good when parked surreptitiously on my latest

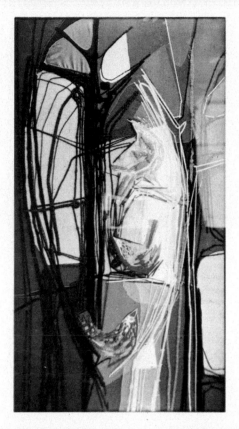

V *Three Birds in a Tree:* by Diana Springall
(Property of the Inner London Education Authority)

semi-realistic creations—and my fishes took on the wrong sort of surrealism when their tails were removed and placed in their mouths—so I started to play about with abstract shapes. This particular picture started off with placing the brilliant pink felt hatchet shapes with paler pink velvet added, on to a deep red ground covered with pink net. Purple felt and velvet shapes were added and white and vermilion stitches. A friend of mine says that to her the result evokes a feeling of the designs in the Lascaux Caves.

"Tiger in the Jungle" (Plate 11) has a brilliant orange tiger with black net, pale yellow wool and black silk stripes. Bright green felts and varied tones of silk and satin have been used for foliage, and the flowers are in vivid pinks, purples, yellow and white.

For those who cannot always venture out of doors it might help to take a tip from Gainsborough, who composed designs for his landscapes by placing certain objects on his table, such as pieces of cork or coal for his foregrounds—sand and clay for middle grounds, mosses and lichens representing bushes—and broccoli to represent distant woods—also, broken stones for rocks, dried herbs for trees, and pieces of looking-glass for water. These he used as a stimulus to his imagination, magnifying them and improving upon their suggested shapes.

When my husband and I were on holiday by the river, I picked several leaves and wild flowers and pressed them carefully for future reference. As we drifted in a rowing boat, very slowly, with the current, all sorts of exciting and unexpected ideas for compositions caught my eye—the twisting roots of a tree by the river's edge forming a kind of cave—the bright green water-weed which had a rhythmic movement and looked like skeins of silk twisting and turning—five bright blue dragonflies darting to and fro in the brilliant sunlight—small yellow flowers which seemed quite exotic in their jungle-like setting. It is strange how rare, comparatively large, and fascinating these plants can appear from the more unusual view and level of a boat on the river. It is from these experiences that I composed my idea for "The Dragonfly" (Plate 45), which is worked on my grandmother's sixty-year-old hand Singer sewing machine, using black and white cottons. There is some hand embroidery on the pearly pink Lurex wings and in the flower centres. The dragonfly's body and wings have been stitched with glistening green and blue Lurex thread and the flowers are in pinks, reds, oranges and mauves made from silks, velvet and felt. The leaves on the centre branch are of velvet and the ripples on the water are in white machine stitching.

BELDY (Mabel Maugham) is the daughter of Heywood Hardy, the animal painter, and from an early age he taught her the rudiments of drawing and painting. Her father used to give her marks for her work and she recalls a day when he asked her to copy a picture of a sow and her litter. When she handed it to him he reprimanded her because there was one piglet missing in her rendering. She burst into tears because even at that age she knew it didn't really matter—to her it was the impression that counted but to him it was a fault, as a copy demanded

12 *Rotten Row:* by Beldy

13 *A Street in Paris:* by Beldy

meticulous detail. It was interesting that the conventional outlook of the day was dismissed by her in this way at an early age.

When she was 8 years old, Whistler said (after looking at her enchanting and remarkable sketches and water colours) "We shall certainly hear of her one day" and proclaimed her as a child genius.

She had a facility for learning to play on a variety of musical instruments including the piano, zither, guitar and cantele (a Finnish national instrument). This helped to colour her whole future outlook and gave an added experience that all music gives to painters. Musicians have remarked that one can "feel the music" in her pictures.

Her present method of picture making began when she missed a train and sat in the waiting room thinking about how she would repair some cushions. Later, gathering some pieces of varied tones of grey material, she began to patch one and found herself forming cloud shapes. She then thought this was an amusing pastime and made some fish with varied coloured materials on a linen background. Felix Casorate, the painter, saw these first attempts and at once saw future possibilities in them. He suggested that they should be framed and not used for material decorations. He told her to take no notice of what people might say but to go on experimenting. In this way she passed through various phases until she gradually evolved her present style, which gives the effect of an Impressionist painting. She believes that if all ideas of needlework and decorative conceptions are put aside and materials properly used and blended in a painting fashion, they can give results every bit as interesting as oil paint, gouache or water colour.

Beldy has created hundreds of pictures using the guiding principles of colour, values, perspective, impression and movement. She rejects superfluous details and meticulously defined features. She uses fine gauze which she frequently dyes herself for the subtle colours and effects which she requires to "lose" outlines, act as a "glaze" or to convey shadows. Her colours can be sombre and muted or sing with a glowing intensity. Sometimes it will take hours of searching to achieve the exact colour she wants, even though she has a "palette" of over fifty whites—it may often be a piece of faded linen which fits the purpose!

There is an amusing story about someone who bought one of Beldy's pictures and was curious to know exactly how they were done. So she (the buyer) proceeded systematically to pick all the tissues off so that they fell apart like butterfly's wings. Having stripped them off so that nothing was left except the bare canvas, she remained more puzzled than before. This little tale aptly illustrates that underneath it all it's the idea that counts.

Among her many subjects Beldy has portrayed the Stations of the Cross and other religious themes, often in the form of "fabric stained glass windows" like "St Blaise and the Animals" which is made from silk, chiffon and velvet in blues, yellows, greens and rich browns. The animals include lions, bears, otters, a bird and a deer. Three black horizontal bars which go across the picture and thin black lines of silk crossing the animals and trees give the impression of the black leading which holds stained glass window pieces and lends a fascinating flowing effect.

Other themes are landscapes, including the River Seine in its various moods throughout the seasons, and all kinds of animal and figure studies. One picture "Cat in the Alley" shows a mysteriously dark alley-way with a lean cat sitting and peering at the lighter end where a few shops come into view. It is a good example of the atmosphere which Beldy is so good at catching and evoking—the dirty streets reflecting misery and torment—the bright ones showing happiness and contentment. She has designed numerous scenes from the ballet, watching the performance several times, then going away and making an "impression" of movement and atmosphere. The dancers wear white chiffon and silk dresses and convey a light, airy and fluttering sensation.

Her work was first exhibited in 1929 in a mixed exhibition in the Salon des Arts Décoratifs in Paris. One man shows have been held in Italy (Milan, Turin, Rome), Switzerland (Basle, Geneva), France (Paris), America (Boston, New York), and England (London, five exhibitions at the Leicester Galleries). Her pictures have been purchased by the Victoria and Albert Museum and the Manchester Art Gallery.

"In Rotten Row" (Plate 12). Layers of grey material convey the entertaining play and patterns of shadows. As in all her works this was conceived as a painting and executed on canvas. The trees have been handled in such a manner that the glowing sensation of wind-carried leaves is ably suggested. This movement is echoed in the sense of rhythms achieved in the portrayal of the horses and their legs.

In "A Street in Paris" (Plate 13), the suggestion of drizzle and the greyness of a rainy day has been wonderfully conveyed. The shapes of the trees, like umbrella spokes, echo the pattern of the umbrellas which play against the pattern of the shadows from people walking to and fro along the pavement. Varied greys are laid over some of the figures to create the illusion of "form". Here and there a few pencil marks help to express and lend extra depth and intensity to the form. She captures the atmosphere of Paris. This picture was shown in her recent exhibitions at the Grosvenor Gallery.

ELLEN HALLETT studied at the West of England College of Art and has worked in water colour, oils, etching, silverwork and fabric collage She has exhibited in mixed exhibitions including the Society of Women Artists' exhibitions, S.E.A. "Pictures for Schools" and the Medici Gallery, and her work has been purchased by Derbyshire Education Committee Museum Service and shown in B.B.C. television programmes. She was educated at Fairfield Grammar School, Bristol, where she now teaches art.

Her attitude to fabric pictures is that they are a medium on their own and not "half-done embroidery pictures". That whereas embroidery seeks to decorate, enrich or elaborate a piece of plain or partly-textured material, "stuck pictures" make use of a variety of interesting textures and weaving which would not necessarily be suitable to embroider upon.

"Wartime Winter" (Plate 5) was made in 1941 when Ellen Hallett first used the fabric medium. She used bits and pieces kept over from the loose covers her sisters

14 *Babylon Riding the Great Dragon:*
by Elizabeth Allen

15 *Snow:* by Ellen Hallett

16 *Figurehead* (Marlborough): by Gerald Holtam
(*In the Royal Naval Engineering College, Maradon*)

17 *Saints:* by Gerald Holtam
(*In the church of St Oswald and St Aiden, Coventry*)

had made and became so absorbed in her creations that it helped to take her mind off the air-raids. The scene is based on a view as seen from across her room. It is an example of a familiar view reminiscent of many which everyone has seen at one time or another, rendered delightfully and with an original twist by her clever use of materials. The predominant colours are warm browns, cool greys and white. Velour, cretonne and hessian furnishing fabrics form the foreground surface textures. The snow shadows and footprints are in blue organdie.

"Spring" (Plate 4) was an imaginary landscape prompted by the memory of country walks during that season. Various shades of green and brown furnishing fabrics (some purposely frayed) were used in the foreground and middle distance. Cotton wool, net and organdie formed the cloud shapes. The gate was of patterned cretonne, catkins of silver oiled silk, branches of brown corduroy velvet crash. Materials used for the middleground were chosen not only for colour and tone but for their particular weave and surface texture, contrasting with the almost plain surfaces of the fore and backgrounds.

Her delightful fabric collage, "Snow", (Plate 15), was an imaginary snow-scene prompted by country walks in the snow. Apart from white, the colours in it are mainly greys, oranges and browns. The sky and distant hills are of grey Harris tweed with "washes" of blue and white organdie. The roofs are chiefly of hucka-back, Saxony cloth and piqué, overlaid in places by blue organdie. The walls of houses are of orange-brown cretonne, and trees, hedgerows, etc., are of grey and brown sateen. The various shapes were cut out direct from different materials arranged and rearranged, then pinned on to canvas stretched over cardboard. These shapes were then removed and stuck firmly in position from memory, beginning with the sky and ground and continuing with the larger shapes. The details were added last. No stitching was used and no preliminary "rough" drawing was made either in pencil or cut paper. The picture was made in 1944, added to later and exhibited in the Society of Women Artists' Exhibition in 1950. The late T. W. Earp commented on the work in the *Daily Telegraph* saying that "E. K. Hallett's patchwork 'Snow Pattern'" (as it was originally called) "had the charm of a Klee picture."

GERALD HOLTAM trained as a painter at the Royal College of Art where he met his wife, Madeleine E. Anderson, who is also a painter. Before turning to work in fabric he was a furniture designer and still is a fabric designer, having his own work-shop for the production of textiles. The work at the College of the late Frank Barber who did stained glass and fabric murals stimulated him; it was the first time he had seen materials used in such an interesting and inventive way. Years later he decided to try his hand at large works involving the application of fabric and these have included proscenium curtains and giant wall-hangings especially commissioned for schools and churches all over the British Isles. Designs for some of these have arisen out of the names or associations of the places concerned. He has been assisted by David Holt and they have both designed and executed their own ideas.

Heavy linens which can take the weight of applied materials are used for backgrounds and the various pieces are sewn on with an electric trade machine. Textiles especially designed from his workshop are often incorporated and exciting effects are achieved with gold and silver which catch the light and make rich contrasts.

"Marlborough" (Plate 16) is one of a set of fabric figureheads at the Royal Naval Engineering College, Maradon. The whole figure measures 13 feet high by 8 feet across. The face alone is 4 feet 6 inches high and is made of unbleached linen with brown, grey and green cloth placed upon it and the features outlined with 3- and 6-ply wool. The eyes (which are in orange linen and make a contrast with some of the others made from silver and sequins to give them additional glitter) are practically the size of dinner plates. The wig is in pale purple. Four tones of deep blue specially printed fabric by Gerald Holtam forms a rich background. While he was working on the figurehead commission he found that research while being interesting can often have its more trying moments. The rain simply pelted down his back while he was sketching in the Plymouth dockyard, until a representative of Her Majesty's Navy helpfully appeared with a large umbrella which he obligingly held over his head until the figurehead drawing was made!

A particularly interesting religious hanging is behind the altar in a church designed by Basil Spence at Coventry. It is 26 feet high by 18 feet across and is based on the story of St Oswald and St Aiden. King Oswald gave food to the poor on a Celtic silver dish and because of his kindness St Aiden touched his right arm and said, "May this arm never perish." Later, the king's arm was cut off in battle, but true to the wish, it never perished.

In the fabric hanging (Plate 17) St Oswald's right arm is in red material. St Aiden has a silver face and hands (a convention of Gerald Holtam's for celestial figures). The colouring is very rich, viridian green, purple and vermilion linen, crimson velvet, "shocking pink" wool and gold and silver leaf. The stylized shapes round the figures are in white linen.

GWYNFA JONES was taught by Margaret Kaye at Birmingham College of Art and later studied at the Royal College of Art. After teaching at the Medway College of Art and at Camberwell School of Art, she went to St Martin's School of Art where she taught experimental design and machine embroidery until she left to look after her small son. She has exhibited at the Medici Gallery and at the Society for Education in Art "Pictures for Schools" exhibitions.

A machined picture, "Interior with Fish" (not shown), has an acid yellow cotton background. The trailing plants are in dark green gauze with pale blue, black and red organzas which overlap in places and being transparent produce extra colours. The fish is in green silk gauze with black sequins and a machined backbone. A large quantity of black millinery veiling can be seen and this overlaps the yellow mount in an original way. The striped material makes a most fitting wallpaper and it is interesting to see the machined fan-shaped decoration worked over the door.

"Fishes" (Plate 19) had a sulphurous green background. White net under purple net forms the body of one fish, with pink and yellow net spots for pattern. The

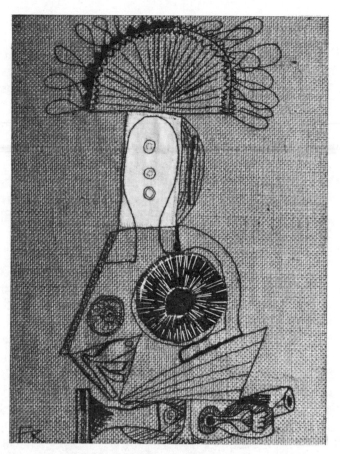

18 *Rosette:* by Frances Richards

19 *Fishes:* by Gwynfa Jones

other fish is yellow organza with white organdie and pink and black net with white machined patterns. The black and grey nets and gauzes of various sized meshes and the sulphurous greens and purples help to convey the dark mysterious quality of a sea bed.

JOSEPHINE JORDAN studied painting and embroidery at Goldsmiths' College of Art. She is married to a structural engineer and teaches art at Croydon High School. She exhibits in the Society for Education in Art "Pictures for Schools" and the Society of Designer Craftsmen's exhibitions. Her fabric pictures can be compared to stained glass in richness and impact, and these are the qualities she found were missing when she worked in the medium of oil paint. She often chooses dark backgrounds and her designs very cleverly emerge from out of them and are not lost in general tone.

The idea for "Henry VIII" (Plate III) came very quickly and clearly and took just about an hour to design on paper. His costume, character and wonderful square shape appealed to her imagination. This is an example of a picture which does not have such a dark background but it is still near in tone to the main figure. The patterned background is achieved by lines of black felt stitched on to the blue cotton background and rows of black silk embroidered in coral stitch. Other fabrics used are coloured velvet, cotton, silk, a gold and blue patterned material and a white ribbed silk. Black wool and gold thread have been used in various forms of stitchery—couching, cross stitch, coral stitch, chain stitch, feather stitch and herring-bone stitch. Black beads and beads with a purple and yellow glow enrich the stitches and have been used for patterns on the sleeves, the hat and down the centre panel. For additional interest, the face has been "broken up" into three different colours and textures.

MARGARET KAYE studied stained glass at the Royal College of Art. Her husband is Reece Pemberton, who is a free-lance stage designer. She teaches at Camberwell School of Art.

It is apparent that her training in stained glass has greatly influenced her approach to fabric pictures as she uses a mixture of tweed, wool, felt and silk so that she achieves an effect of glowing light which can also be seen in pieces of built-up stained glass. The pieces are placed in layers which are cut smaller each time so that one vibrates against another. There is no sticking and the fabric shapes are roughly stitched together in a completely unorthodox way, which is probably why the results are so delightfully fresh. There is no danger of her stitching becoming too "precious" as she is reputed to have said that as regards domestic sewing she can just about sew a button on a coat and that is all. The wools and silks give the effect of a free and vigorous drawing. There is a similarity in the rich and exuberant juxtaposition of colours and patterns which appear in the collages made by Margaret Kaye and the tapestries designed by Jean Lurçat. The dramatic intensity which is achieved by both of them would be difficult to equal in oil-paint.

The introduction to the catalogue for her first exhibition at Roland Browse and

20 *Sun Caught in a Tree:* by Jean Carter

Delbanco says: "M. Kaye's delight in material and surface, the discovery of the expressive possibilities of yarn and thread and the finding of beauty in a neglected remnant is not unlike Gris' and Schwitter's ecstasy in a sample of wallpaper. Her animals are the happy result of a sensitive feeling for grafting diverse fabrics on to each other; they are not translations from oil paintings into textiles, the stuff (*la matiere*) of which they are made contributes as much to our enjoyment as the design. They have the sphinx-like fascination of being half-object, half-image."

Margaret Kaye rarely makes a preliminary sketch for her work. She buys a background, spreads it out flat, brings out her rag-bags (some of which contain clippings from materials that made up theatrical wardrobes) and lays pieces of colour over it. When she has decided what she will use she gradually builds up the shapes by cutting out patches of contrasting colours in contrasting materials from tweeds, wools, felts and a small amount of silk. She has now had four exhibitions at Roland, Browse and Delbanco and it is interesting to note the progress she has made since her first show. Her "Bull and Pigeons", which is in the collection of the Victoria and Albert Museum, has a pictorial effect in that the shapes are outlined or silhouetted against the background. Later works show a natural transition to a more unified, painterly conception. Now the applied shapes "sink" into the background.

"The Owl with Moths" (Frontispiece) illustrates the wit with which she spices her pictures which have a strange, fanciful quality. The concave beak gives just that originality and humour which the conventional convex shape would lack; the different colours of the eyes produce two different levels in perspective and makes them appear to twinkle in a mischievous manner at the circling moths; these effects, half intuitive, half planned, are always unexpected and exciting. The rust colour on one foot which is carried through on to the wings lends a warmth to the picture which would have been lost if the subtle coolness of the white and beiges had been unrelieved. The pieces of blue satin on the darker background shine like jewels in a mosaic.

ROGER BANKS has been described as a "somewhat eccentric young man who lives by himself in a medieval castle, shooting pigeons in the deserted ballrooms for his meals".

One afternoon at an Adult Education College he found himself hustled into a room by an animated wooden-beaded lady who might have passed for Miss Philomela Poppyseed herself, and was excitedly instructed to "Let your material *speak* to you!" He gave one look at the cascade of rags and wondered how long it was till lunch—but three years in the Antarctic, spent in continual preoccupation with the textures of snow and ice, had subconsciously prepared him not only for painting pictures and writing a book on "The Unrelenting Ice", but for working in fabric collages and he began to see endless possibilities in the medium.

He debunks any idea that people should approach Art with "Church faces" and prefers to see his work hung in the nursery, bathroom, or propped on the odd kitchen shelf to make people feel gay. His "kitchen sink" collages ("Fishes" and

21 *Puffing Billy:* by Roger Banks

22 *Girl in the Square:* by Kathleen Mills

"Fowls" e.g. a "Turkey" with goosepimples larger than life made out of seer-sucker) combine the witty touch which is apparent in his approach as a culinary artist and a graphic designer.

"Puffing Billy" (Plate 21) has net curtain material for the steam, braid is used for the roof of the shelter, "bunched up" lace for a passenger's collar and pleated silk material to give a three-dimensional effect for the skirt. All the pieces are stuck with Copydex on to hardboard.

KATHLEEN MILLS studied dress, millinery and theatrical design at Sheffield College of Art, and dress design at the Royal College of Art. She now teaches dress design and general art and craft subjects at the Sheffield College of Art. She has exhibited at the Crafts Centre, the "Crafts Today" exhibition and the Society for Education in Art "Pictures for Schools" exhibition. Her earlier fabric pictures were delicately stitched in hand embroidery. The later ones have been executed with an electric Singer sewing machine. She has sketch books filled with drawings for reference—architecture, plants and so on. She sometimes does a pen and ink drawing before commencing a picture but usually works an idea out freely straight away with the fabrics and sewing machine, making no marks whatever on any of the fabrics as she dislikes working to a set layout. Her recurring subjects include wood-sprites, houses, fishes and abstract designs, using such materials as gauze and net over felt shapes stitched on to a felt background or black machine lines on a felt background with a jewel in the centre.

"Girl in the Square" is reminiscent in style of some contemporary Italian paintings (Plate 22). It has a pink sky with grey, yellow and lavender buildings. The ground is grey, the figure is coffee-coloured silk and the dress is pink silk threaded with gold Lurex. The stitching is in black and white. Other colours on the houses are lavender, grey, dull pink, pale acid green and pale yellow. One picture "Early Locomotive", based on Stephenson's "Rocket", was made entirely of black, orange, red and yellow felts on a turquoise background. Wheels were made of curtain rings with sequins in the centre and bugle beads for door handles. The black machine stitches pick out the drawing. A beguiling picture, "A Partridge in a Pear Tree", has a red ground which is cut away to show the simple horizontal spiked branches of a dark green tree with a few narrow oval leaves. The whole picture has a charming simplicity. The bird is in the form of a triangle, which is larger at the bottom, with rounded corners. A few running stitches alternate with rows of jewels on the body, tail and wing. Two jewel eyes and a felt beak complete the partridge. The pears have sequins on the bottom of them.

"Girl and Moon", in yellow silk with black machine stitching, shows a large moon depicted by circles which get larger and larger, and leafy hot-house plants with a three-quarter-length figure clad in a decorative shift.

JOHN NOBLE trained as an illustrator at Goldsmiths' College of Art and St Martin's School of Art. He worked in a theatre workshop for two years and has done several window displays.

24 *Madonna and Rose*: by John Noble

23 *Mermaid*: by John Noble

"Madonna and Child" (Plate 10) was suggested by a reproduction of a Russian icon. The faces are painted in pale green water colour on a rich reddish-brown silk. Much of the material and jewellery used has been procured from junk shops. The background and other fabrics are in various types of gold cloth. Paste diamonds, pearls, sequins and trimmings, together with a brooch, enrich the figures. Gold braid is used for the outer "frame". The stitching is for the most part practically invisible.

"The Mermaid" (Plate 23) is a portrait which is larger than life-size—at least I think so judging from the last mermaid I saw! The face is made from duck-egg blue corduroy, pearls and corals form the necklace and the hair is pale green silk. An illusion of water is created by green net while sequins suggest sea-spray. Pink and red silks and white and silver Lurex material make up the garland round her head. Chain stitch, blanket stitch and couching have been used.

After completing a few tapestry pictures he turned to fabric-picture-making. "Madonna and Rose" (Plate 24) was based on 18th-century wax figures which he saw, admired and could not afford to buy. The figures, which had painted faces, glass eyes and real hair, were dressed in the then height of fashion in clothes made from brocade, lace and tinsel and at that time it was the custom for a baby boy to be dressed in girl's clothes until he grew old enough to wear a small version of a man's costume. Behind the figures there was a painted background and in front a delicately carved wooden balcony with a small urn of cambric flowers. The fabric picture is in subdued shades of brown, beige and grey. The child's dress is in lace with bows of cream baby ribbon and mushroom velvet. The faces are in water colour painted on grey satin and real hair has been used. The rose is a small artificial one. Both figures have chain stitch outlines.

FRANCES RICHARDS studied design at the Royal College of Art and met her husband, Ceri Richards the painter, there. During her course there she, too, was very fascinated with the murals which Frank Barber, the same artist who influenced Gerald Holtam, was making entirely out of pieces of fabric. This was her first introduction to the medium as used in the 20th century. Some years later when she was teaching pottery design at Camberwell School of Art, a London County Council Art Inspector asked her if she would give some lectures on embroidery design, with the emphasis on design, to the two-year training students at Goldsmiths' College. She knew little of actual embroidery stitches but, realizing that some examples would have to be shown, she made three pictures, all portraits, in velvets on linen. One of them was of her eldest daughter, Rachel. She used darning stitch, backstitch and couched-on pieces of braid which gave a rich, bold appearance and were very stimulating to the students who had not seen anything like them before and were thrilled with the idea of trying out designs for themselves. Sir Colin Anderson happened to see them when he visited her husband about his paintings and asked if she would carry out a mural 6 feet by 4 feet for the liner *Orcades*. Shortly after leaving the Royal College of Art, Frances Richards illustrated *The Book of Revelation* with lithographs (published by Faber). All had black outlines

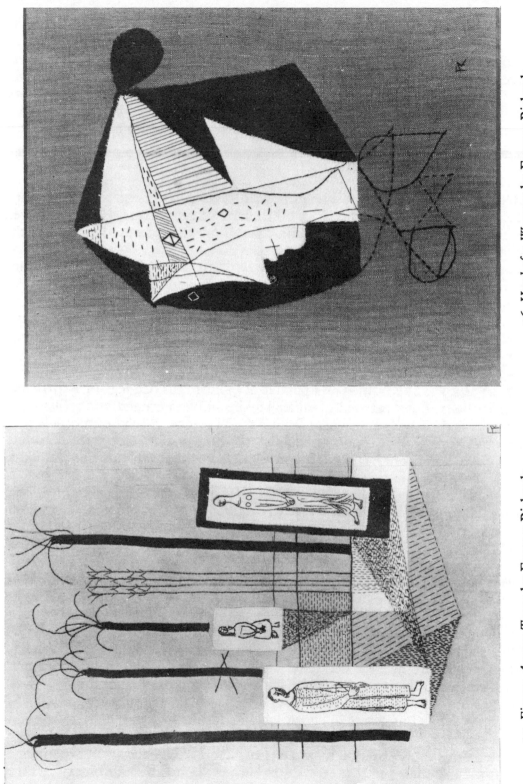

26 *Head of a Woman*: by Frances Richards
(In the collection of the Hon. Mrs Lucille Frost)

25 *Figures Among Trees*: by Frances Richards
(In the collection of Sir Colin Anderson)

and possessed a strong linear quality which seems to have influenced her fabric pictures. Her works are austere and poetical, as can be seen in "Figures among Trees" (Plate 25). This has a linen background with black trees. The figures are portrayed in an original way on rectangular shapes and worked in very fine black running stitches. The stylised shadows are in dark blue, brown and black. These make an interesting link between the three rectangles.

"Head of a Woman" (Plate 26) is in vandyke brown, black, white, grey-blue and indigo blue lines.

"Rosette" (Plate 18) is on a brown hessian ground with white rayon forming the face and pieces of black rayon in other parts of the picture. Red silk is used with black on the mouth and the same colours for the rosette. The rest of the hand stitching, minutely detailed, is in black.

She has had four exhibitions, three at the Redfern Gallery and one at the Hanover. Her pictures have been bought by the Victoria and Albert Museum and by several educational authorities. She has designed figures for an altar frontal in colourings of gold, white and yellow, when her fabric medium was incorporated in "Art in Craftsmanship" for the ecclesiastical exhibition held in the Smithsonian Institution in Washington.

CHRISTINE RISLEY trained as a painter at Goldsmiths' College of Art. It was there that she met and married Norman Jenkinson, who trained as an illustrator and teaches at the London School of Printing. She teaches machine embroidery at Goldsmiths' College of Art and design and machine embroidery at St Martin's School of Art. Her work has been in several mixed exhibitions and she has had a one-man show at the Hanover Gallery.

A criticism about her show in *Art News and Review* mentioned her as "A very assured manipulator of fabric collage. Rich colour, a great deal of feminine whimsicality and prodigious skill combine to make these pictures not only wonderfully pretty but also formally satisfying." Dora Billington wrote in *The Studio*, "Christine Risley uses her materials in well-defined shapes making good surface patterns, a considerable range of tones and a certain amount of perspective in pleasant painter-like compositions. The patches are held together with the minimum of sewing, but by varying the size of stitches and the thickness of thread she achieves with considerable economy some very expressive drawing."

When she was studying painting she was always interested in design and arranging shapes of colour against each other and did not care for meticulous drawing. She turned to fabric pictures because she loved using different textures and the fabric medium gave the widest choice of all.

She enjoys spending hours in shops looking at and selecting fabrics, boxes of sequins, beads and feathers, and when her purchases are spread out in her workroom they serve as an inspiration for another picture. She believes in experimenting with the materials and that they should not be limited to embroidery pictures but that there is a great future in the use of pure collage with no stitching at all.

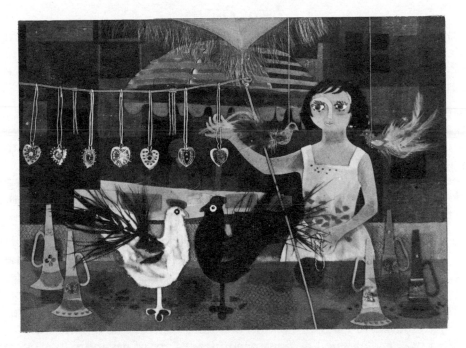

27 *Children's Toys in the Market, Yugoslavia:* by Christine Risley

28 *The Fish:* by Rosa Branson

She thinks that some fabrics naturally fray at the edges, that this is typical of the substance and should be incorporated in that way with no attempts at camouflage. Each new picture is tackled with a fresh approach. Her work has fallen into roughly three periods:

(i) using a lot of fine embroidery to emphasize shapes and textures on delicate chiffon and organdie materials,

(ii) a middle period using much less embroidery and presenting a fine tissue or papery quality,

(iii) her present style which combines the contrasting weights of felts, organdies, and silks and relies on small pieces of material cut out to emphasize texture and pattern rather than on using a great deal of stitching.

"The Midsummer Fairy" (not shown) has a background made of rayon taffeta. Felt with layers of organdie made the dress. The face and hands are pink silk. (The material from the arm with the hand holding the wand has been laid over a continuation of the orange felt cut in the same shape so that no puckers are made and a smooth line is maintained.) The hair is small pieces of yellow-gold silk on yellow cotton. The clouds are made of net and organdie while a fine nylon straw gives the misty effect over the moon. The flowers and leaves are of organdie, cotton, silk and velvet. The materials have been "caught down" with minute matching stitches. The wings are in fine gold striped material with various coloured beads and sequins added. Feather stitch has been used in the leaves. French knots decorate the dress and the pattern on the wings is couched in fine black thread.

"Owl and House" (Plate 6), was inspired by an owl in a glass case owned by the artist. The house is from a model in Blackheath Park. The owl is ochre-coloured against a dark khaki green tree with a pink and dark red house. The sky is of grey-green bits of shantung from Christine Risley's wedding dress. The back of the tree is particularly intriguing with its pattern formation and use of tone.

"Woman and Birds" (Plate 7) has a contrast of felts and organdies—a pale turquoise blue background with pinks, greens, black and pearly grey. The woman has orange hair which makes a change from conventional colouring.

"Children's toys in the market, Yugoslavia" (Plate 27) was from an actual holiday scene. The use of the abstract design of printed pale and dark grey squares on cotton is particularly interesting, with here and there squares of black organdie and purple net superimposed, giving an illusion of houses in the background. The green-yellow stripes on the umbrella have been stuck on and green net in front with darker stripes on the right gives a shadowed effect. The girl's hair and the feathers on the birds' bodies have been stuck on in mosaic-like chunks. These are made of black velvet and felt for the hair (on a beige cotton shape) and black and dark reddish-purple velvet on a copper-coloured silk for the bird on the right. Real gaily coloured feathers in pinks, vivid vermilion and pale yellow lend an amusing touch to the other birds. Lockets are in varying materials containing silver and gold. Very few stitches are used and some of the materials are stuck down.

29 *Quarry:* by Bernice Carlill
(Property of the West Sussex Education Committee)

30 *City Lights:* by Lisa MacDonogh

BERNICE CARLILL studied painting at the Slade. She married a childhood friend, Desmond Carlill, who is a physiologist, and she taught for some years in secondary schools for girls. She left to look after her small son, Ceri, and tried to carry on with her painting. Nappies and general baby routine refused to co-operate with oil-paints and brushes, and she couldn't concentrate long enough to get anywhere with a painting, so she turned to the fabric medium. This is safer where curious toddlers are concerned, it could be picked up easily at odd moments and opened out a new vision for her.

Both her paintings and fabric pictures have the lyrical and poetical approach of the Welsh people. She uses a lot of coloured nets which give a delicate impression of the glazes she used when oil painting. The finished works, however, are more akin to the transparency of watercolours, and the single thread simple stitchery (usually stem stitch) which she uses, portrays a feeling of fine lines used in etching.

When in Wales she sketched a "quarry face with rocks", and later translated the idea into fabrics, using oranges, beiges, yellows and greys in cotton and rayon with "straight" stitching to emphasise some of the forms (Plate 29).

LISA MACDONOGH studied at Chelsea School of Art where she took her Intermediate Examination. She left to get married, and when her three children had reached school age she went to Goldsmiths' College of Art to do painting for the National Diploma in Design and to obtain her Art Teachers' Certificate. She had previously experimented with batik using wax on cloth and dyeing it. After doing appliqué on the Teachers' Course, she combined the two, concentrating on the play of light which could be seen when the work was held up to the window. Carrying it further she isolated certain shapes by masking the back of the picture with felt, so that other parts shone through, resulting in a very beautiful translucent quality somewhat akin to stained glass.

"City Lights" (Plate 30) is designed in this way in vivid pinks and oranges, with the addition of lurex and rafia in the same colours. Other abstract subjects have been "Microcosm" and "Amoeba in Spring".

She feels that the fabric medium is, as yet, not taken seriously enough as a work of art. There is still a certain amount of snob value attached to the oil-painting medium however mediocre some of the paintings may be, and a tendency to forget that it is the *design* that counts primarily, not the *technique*.

EIRIAN SHORT studied sculpture at Goldsmiths' College of Art and met her husband Denys Short, a painter, during her training. He contributes to her work by giving her his old shirts and socks (a bottle-green one made a very convincing monkey puzzle tree). Eirian Short became interested in hand embroidery and later took lessons in trade machine work at Barrett Street Technical College. She teaches machine embroidery at Hornsey School of Art and at Goldsmiths' College of Art. She is an associate member of the Crafts Centre and has shown her work in several mixed exhibitions including the Society of Designer Craftsmen's exhibitions, the Society for Education in Art "Pictures for Schools", Travelling Arts Council

31 *Abstract, based on a Rose:* by Eirian Short
(*Property of the Embroiderers' Guild*)

32 *Hermon Chapel:*
by Eirian Short

Exhibition, Women's International Exhibition, and the Medici Gallery. Her work has been purchased for the Schools Service in the National Museum of Wales.

There is a sculptural quality about "Abstract based on a Rose" (Plate 31). The background is off-white Indian cotton with a rough weave and dark brown felt is used for the other shapes. Stitches are "running", "couching", "raised chain band" and "backstitch wheel" worked in embroidery cottons of various thicknesses.

"Hermon Chapel" (Plate 32) is based on various buildings she has seen in Cardiganshire. It has been almost entirely worked on a Jones sewing machine. The mottled pink and grey cotton used for the chapel gives an effect of stone. All the machine stitches are in black or white thread, and can be seen on the windows, railings (satin stitch), tree bark, the decoration on the top of the chapel, round the moon and the pebbles. The choice of colour contrasting excitingly with a navy background helps to create the illusion of night.

ANNE GILLESPIE SMITH took painting for her National Diploma in Design at Kingston upon Thames School of Art and her Art Teacher's Certificate at Goldsmiths' College of Art, where she met her husband, Michael Preston, who is now a free-lance artist and art teacher. While she was at Goldsmiths' she went to embroidery classes with some trepidation, knowing they would be useful but feeling rather tentative about it all because she was sure that she couldn't do anything which required neatness and precision. The only stitches she knew were adapted versions of tacking and running stitch. When she started her first fabric picture she was suddenly intrigued by the decorative possibilities of the medium, the wide range in the textures and the brilliance of many synthetic materials. She found that the basic design mattered far more than she had ever anticipated and the technique and stitches far less. The latter were learnt by cobbling away happily on the corner of the picture where it didn't show. She began to enjoy the discipline imposed on her by the use of a pair of scissors, and the fact that simplicity came first, followed by elaboration, and not vice versa. She feels that this type of work has almost unlimited possibilities and that the bad work which is sometimes seen is not due to any fault in the medium but to lack of sufficient designing, allied to slovenly technique. She is a member of the Society of Designer Craftsmen and the Embroiderers' Guild and has exhibited with the Arts and Crafts Exhibitions Society, "Pictures for Schools", the Medici Gallery, at the Crafts Centre and in other mixed exhibitions. Her work has been purchased by the National Museum of Wales, the Embroiderers' Guild and several education authorities. She teaches at Berridge House and Bromley High School.

She loves cats but is allergic to them so cannot possess one and to make up for it a little she creates fabric pictures of them. "Cat and Kitten" (Plate 33), grew from watching a friend's cat smugly contemplating her sleeping family. The background is yellow linen. Both cats are white with pink noses made from ribbed material and pink ears. The eyes are made from black velvet and all the stitching is black except for the stars which are pale pink.

33 *Cat and Kitten:* by Anne Gillespie Smith

34 *Sunflowers:* by Shirley Stone

SHIRLEY STONE studied at the Woolwich School of Art and later at the Royal College of Art. She obtained her Diploma in textile design. She has taught textile design, fabric printing and weaving at Chelmsford, Dagenham and Southend Schools of Art. She exhibits with the Society for Education in Art "Pictures for Schools" exhibition. Her first fabric collage was produced while she was still a student and on holiday in Looe, Cornwall. She felt there that water colours did not satisfy her feelings about the rich strong colour around her. It came naturally to her to use a fabric because being a textile designer she handled fabrics more than paint and it seemed an appropriate material for pictorial work. She usually chooses to design from drawings of subjects she has seen, although occasionally she prefers a purely imaginative theme. Her method has become free over the years.

"Sunflowers" (Plate 34), is an extremely rich design in which rectangular shapes of different coloured nets have been laid and lightly stitched over grey hessian. The long running stitches are in various coloured cottons and small snippets of coloured cottons and silks make up the yellow sunflowers. Beads form the stamens.

"Loading Tunny Fish in Brittany" (Plate 42), has a grey hessian background overlaid with grey, black and white net. The lorry is a dark olive green rayon fabric. The fisherman in the foreground is in pink cotton with a black beret. The woman is completely in black except for a white cap and the men loading the fish are in various dark blues and blacks. One of the boats is pink.

"The Bird" (Plate 43), is almost life size. The background is in red and purple net and the bird is black silk with a black lace wing and head feathers.

JEAN CARTER trained in fabric painting and hand embroidery at the Tunbridge Wells School of Art and Manchester College of Art and Design. She is married to an artist and they are mad about their three cats, a Brown Burmese, Abyssinian, and Russian Blue. She is the Senior Lecturer in Art and Craft at Battersea College of Education, and a member of the Embroiderers' Guild "62 Group". She is fascinated by things (plants, the seashore, etc) colours, fabrics, threads and techniques in embroidery. Her "Sun caught in a Tree" (Plate 20) expresses the emotion she felt with this vision and shows the sense of wonder she experienced at the colours and patterns in nature. A vivid orange and pink sun, caught in the spiky lines of a tree, is worked in couched wools, using machine embroidery.

Her work has been bought by the Embroiderers' Guild, Liverpool Museum, Women's Institute and private collections.

ELIZABETH ALLEN, crippled since birth and in constant pain, trained at an early age as a seamstress. Later, she made decorative pillow-cases and cushion covers and gradually turned from these and started to make her "patchwork pictures" before the First World War.

When she was 80 she thought it was God's will that she should die and made what was to be her last picture, showing herself dead and ready for burial.

She looked upon her works as manifestations of her religion and morality rather than as works of art. Bridget Poole, a young art student, first saw her vast

VI *Mountain Flowers:* by Eugenie Alexander

collection and took some of the College staff to see it; this eventually led to an exhibition of sixty pictures at the Crane Kalman gallery when she was 82. The girl left home and went to look after her in the isolated First War prefab, her home in a wood where she had been living as a recluse. She kept in touch with the world outside by listening to the radio and reading the newspapers where she found much of her material. She has only seen one film and been to the sea once —and was unable to go to the opening of her exhibition.

Her pictures, which belong to the category of "primitive" works, are related in feeling and design to Persian and Mogul miniatures and to certain folk-art embroideries—her ideas are a fantasy of the East, Biblical, fairy tale, Arabian Nights and interpreted newspaper photographs.

Her pictures have a rich "antique" appearance with the use of faded silks and satins shredded with age. Suede, flannel, pieces of patterned material (for flowers and trees) beads and sequins appear constantly and glowing reds, purples and greens are also often used.

In "Babylon Riding the Great Dragon" (Plate 14) she uses couching, blanket, and chain stitch to outline the figures and building—thick lace is used on the latter to form a decorative feature.

ROSA BRANSON went to the Slade (to study painting) and Camberwell ("Design" with Margaret Kaye).

She alternates her collage work with painting and in each is seeking to portray effects of light. She spent two years intermittently copying Turner paintings in the National Gallery, and also studied and took up Persian embroidery, teaching herself from observation.

In her collage work she achieves the impression of the painter's "glazes" with fine nets. She often works on the floor, placing the large background material or canvas on the carpet, pinning through into it and securing the pieces with near-invisible stitches in self-matching cotton threads. She is apt to work in batches of thirty, going from one picture to another as the gay or sombre mood (reflected in the colours she sometimes uses) takes her.

Her early works (mostly birds) had pieces of net crossing over each other, forming the more subtle background colours, with added pieces of jewel-coloured satins, velvets, and Lurex, and beads and sequins.

Now she is using fewer colours and more tones, and her present work is in a lower key in colouring. "The Fish" (Plate 28) is made from lace and net in black, grey and brown with diamond beads just visible through them. The background is dove-grey and the sun is pale silver and gold covered with pale dove-grey net. It has a mysterious feeling of space as opposed to space in depth.

She has exhibited her collages twice at the Woodstock Gallery and at the "Pictures for Schools" exhibitions. Her work has been bought by education and hospital authorities and several architects.

CHAPTER V

Some Additional Ideas

IN CASE it may be of further help I have selected a few more ideas from pictures of different kinds. First I have listed some ideas from children but have offered no explanation as to their source of inspiration. Sometimes they cannot tell one what actually gave them an idea: it just comes from personal experience or from things imbibed and remembered, and this often results in a glorious galaxy of unselfconscious and magic expressionism. Then I have written a short account of some amateurs' approaches to fabric-picture-making, to show the beginners' viewpoints. Thirdly I have described some more of my own pictures and have attempted to show how they originated and what a trained artist's viewpoint may be.

CHILDREN

The other day I was asked for a list of subjects which would appeal to children to carry out for picture making at home or at school. The following successful ideas chosen by the children themselves were entered in a B.B.C. children's television competition.

(i) "Father pushing pram" by Juliet Golding, aged 4. These were very simple felt shapes, triangles, a rectangle and circles stuck on to a felt background. To the child the triangle and circles represented father and the baby, and the rectangle was the pram. Incidentally the shapes filled the picture space superbly.

(ii) "Boats on the sea" by Simon Heseltine, aged 6. The boats were in light brown corduroy stuck on to a blue taffeta sea. The blue had been stuck on to the background in chunks to give a good impression of waves.

(iii) "Siamese Cat" by Catherine Miles, aged 7. This was a fawn and chestnut velvet textured material on a background made of white lint. Blue ribbon with a white edging was used for the eyes.

(iv) "The Wedding" by Paddy Ann Joyner, aged 7. This was sewn and was very rich, original and amusing. There was a large church of grey cotton on the right with a weather vane, a stained glass window made of coloured silk fabrics and net, the vicar and the bridegroom waiting to receive the bride who was walking up the path with two friends holding her veil. There was a large tree on the left with a man and a woman with her dog scurrying by. The whole picture was alive with feeling for the occasion and with pattern and texture.

(v) "Punch and Judy" by Lyn Swift, aged 8. Wool was used for the hair, the

35 *Owl:* by David Kenevane, aged 8

37 *Stork:* by Susan Gibbs, aged 13

36 *The Wedding:* Group picture by girls aged 15
and 16

background was canvas and striped materials had been used in an ingenious way for the front of the stage.

(vi) "The elephant" by Linda Thomas, aged 8. This was a hand-sewn picture with a grey flannel elephant with lace round his feet, sequins on his head, tinsel for his tail with yellow stitches and tinsel round his trunk.

(vii) "Circus parade" by Barbara Neeve, aged 8. This was a parade of circus personalities, with flags lightly tacked on so that they fluttered out as though in a breeze.

(viii) "Two clowns" by Julia Haigh, aged 12. She made ingenious use of spotted, striped and patterned materials for their costumes. Both clowns had red noses, spots on their faces and hats with bobbles. The larger one in front carried an umbrella and was walking the tight rope. The smaller one in the distance was jumping and carried balloons.

(ix) "Bluebottle's wedding" by Pamela Winspear, aged 13. She was the only one to machine her pieces on to the background. The bluebottles had feathers on their heads and beads and sequins for flowers.

(x) "Leaping fish" by Janet Clements, aged 16. This was a beautifully executed piece of work on a ground of blue cotton covered with pale green net. The design had a Chinese flavour, waves rose in swirls couched in white silk, the yellow fish had a pattern of red sequins on its body, the fins were embroidered in yellow couched silk and "feelers" of small beads were made on top of the head.

(xi) "Hiawatha and the firefly" by Hazel Aldridge, aged 16. The large figure of Hiawatha was in felts and woollen fabrics, a matchstick sword in his scabbard, the firefly was brilliant against a yellow blaze of light in yellow cotton and fir trees were embroidered in dark green silk against the distant hills.

In one Comprehensive School a group of children worked on a large hanging and each child designed a leaf and a bird on a piece of rayon. These were cut out and attached to the main background to give the impression of birds on a tree.

"The Owl" by David Kenevane (Plate 35), aged 8, was entered for a B.B.C. television contest. It has such a lot of charm and is made with simple basic shapes made interesting by the subconscious act of tilting the head. Woollen and cotton pieces are attached by large stitches and buttons are used for the eyes. I was most amused when a journalist came to see me one day about some work for a magazine and on spotting "The Owl" said "I don't think we'd better include that—it's too contemporary for our readers."

Susan Gibbs, aged 13, worked "The Stork" (Plate 37) on a black cotton background which she bleached by submerging it in boiling water and parazone after first binding round the centre shapes tightly with string so that these black parts would be untouched by the bleach. This is a version of the primitive method of tie and dye, except that it is "tie and bleach". Raw edges were machined with running and zig-zag stitches. Chain-stitch, cross-stitch (effectively used for the legs) and couching were embroidered by hand. The fringed head was made from an old white silk scarf. Patterned and plain cottons in purples and mauves were used for the body.

"The Fish" (Plate 38) by Anne King, aged 15, started life as a "doodle". She began by placing the blue felt arrow shape for the tail and built the picture up from there in blue and black felts. On top and between these she "doodled" with the sewing machine and achieved this delightful Chinese kite-like design of solid pieces of felt contrasting with delicate machine stitching.

Phyllis Hyman, who teaches at a school for E.S.N. children, found that the girls would get easily bored and frustrated with *stitching* pieces of material but were thrilled to *stick* all the pieces down with Copydex.

Several delightful fabric pictures were made in limited colours (black, white, yellow and red) from tweeds and woollen materials. They were adapted from their paintings of "Newsboys" which Phyllis Hyman had previously introduced by acting the idea in front of the class, mentioning buses, busy street atmosphere, etc. She found that where these girls were concerned, after several cut-paper pictures had been made, it was a far easier step to the fabric medium.

Later, one of the girls painted a "Wedding" and Plate 36, an ambitious group project which was highly successful (12 girls taking part), is based on this design. After a lack of enthusiasm at the beginning, one of the girls started to make the "bride" and then everyone wanted a hand in it. One girl painstakingly cut out all the flowers from what was left of their teacher's nightdress, another (who could hardly cut out at all) made all the tombstones, others chose one or two figures and were solely responsible for them, cutting them out carefully (choosing models from "Vogue" for reference) and putting them between layers of cartridge papers to keep them flat until the picture had reached a stage where they were required. The whole project took a month to complete (working in special lessons and using any spare time available), and the only help the class received from the teacher was with some of the difficult tracing and the arranging of the bride's veil. Pale blue nylon was used for the sky, paisley material for the stained glass, patterned tweed for the church and ground effects.

ADULT BEGINNERS

At the age of 85 Gertrude Bowen enrolled in silversmith and embroidery classes at Chelmsford Art School. Her grand-daughter told me that she has always been an exquisite needlewoman and for years carried out her own original tapestry designs. She made several fabric pictures while she attended Shirley Stone's classes. It is interesting that although she does beautiful embroidery she does not think that fabric pictures should have much stitching. She feels that this can make the picture become too "tasteful" and just an example of beautiful embroidery which can kill the medium by taking the eye away from the general effect of the fabric chosen for the design. It often leads to over-elaboration, and the materials, being specially chosen to achieve the desired effect, should as far as possible "speak for themselves". She prefers a broader outlook, showing line and colour more than intricate stitching. She thinks that it is wonderful to see something emerging from a heap of scraps.

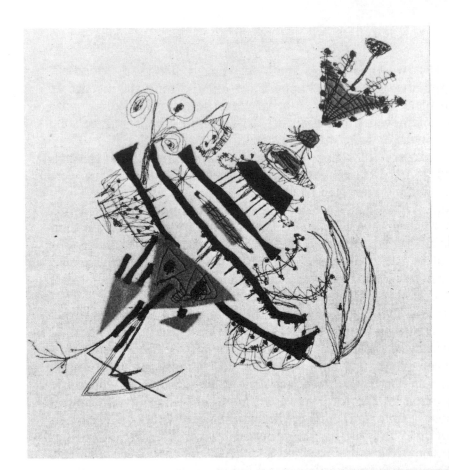

38 *Fish:*
by Anne King, aged 15

39 *Vase of Flowers:*
by Gladys Alexander

"The Spoonbill" (Plate 40), is an original design made entirely from Gertrude Bowen's imagination and inspired by the name of her grand-daughter's sailing boat. It is of no particular place and the bird is her idea of what a spoonbill looks like. Pieces are attached by tacking threads. Overlapping nets, cottons and wools have been used most imaginatively, the patterned cotton material and black lace making very effective rocks. The predominant colours are green, brown, black and purple. Orange felt has been used for the beaks and gives a gay touch.

An earlier picture, "The Owl", was based on a painting by Tunnicliffe. It resembles his work in composition and colour but has been considerably altered by the use of the fabric medium.

My mother, Gladys Alexander, who has a very original mind and used coloured sheets and pillow cases for beds years before anyone else did so, embroidering flowers and initials in each corner of the pillow case and in the centre of the top of the sheets, took to fabric pictures in her fifties. She had done quite a lot of embroidery from transfers, modifying these and using her own stitches and colouring and not being guided by suggestions. These included a map of England with typical products of the island in the shape of animals, wheat and so on. When I first started using fabrics she was secretly smitten with the idea—it was she who had encouraged me to cut out paper figures and so on from magazines and play with them for hours as a child—and one day she presented me with her first fabric picture. She had chosen "The little Mermaid", one of her favourite fairy tales. Using navy blue silk from an old blouse and pale blue linen, a former tray cloth, she formed the sky and the sea. Upon this she laid a piece of lace neatly covering up the join in the horizon line. Her clouds were blue and white spotted muslin. The birds in the sky were copied from those which once decorated the tray cloth. Having got this far she retired to bed. In the middle of the night she had the bright idea that a piece of the underfelt beneath the stair carpet would be the very thing for a rock for the mermaid to sit on. Tearing up the interior of the home is not to be recommended, but it illustrates just how all-absorbing a hobby this can be. She placed it on the right hand side of the picture at the botton, sewed on four shells and went back to bed. Next morning she cut out a fish using a natural history book for reference, and added a ship in full sail cut from a red and white spotted blouse (an old one, this, not still in use!)—and a sailor waving his arms. He was of blue cotton material with a "pom pom" in his hat—obviously a French sailor! The mermaid was gorgeous, if slightly cross-eyed. I am still filled with admiration for her hair which was made from an unplaited yellow silk skein and have never been able to achieve the same effect, try as I may. Her arms are skilfully all but hidden under this magnificent mane. Silver lamé was used for her body with translucent sequins placed in masses on top of each other, and some frayed sacking was used for the tail. To keep her company, sitting on a lump of the rock was a black velvet seal with a pearl eye and woollen whiskers. I have watched seals for hours off Bardsey Island and this one recaptured the squirming, rolling movement which is so typical. He is also clapping his fins and I know my mother used to enjoy seeing

40 *Spoonbill:* by Gertrude Bowen
(*In the collection of Mrs Larcom*)

41 *Spray of Flowers:*
by Alice Johnson

seals do this every year at Bertram Mills' Circus. This gives proof that someone who insists that she "can't draw a thing" *can* do so if she has studied something long enough so that a pose or a movement of a shape is *felt*. Somehow this comes out, and it is bound to do so. The only stitches used in "The little Mermaid" were cross-stitches for the waves, couching for the pattern on the fish, satin stitch for eyes and blanket stitch along the rocks and top of the boat. My father, who had retired from the sea, was so fascinated with her first picture that he persuaded her to make another and allow him to help. The subject was "The Owl and the Pussy Cat" and my father's contribution was the decoration of the sky on which he arranged silver sequins in the form of the Plough on a black silk background. Pieces of blue rayon, sewn together in triangular shapes because there was not enough to use in one whole piece, were the sea and again the horizon was covered, this time with silver Christmas ribbon. A wonderfully textured piece of maple coloured silk was chosen for the beach. This was cut out in a most attractive irregular shape and the edges couched in white wool, fluffed out here and there. Some silver lamé suggested the light from the moon, which was silver and circled with translucent sequins. A boat was placed at a "rocky" angle with a cocktail stick for the mast, and a striped flag attached to it. This sail was more pendant-shaped. A very small lighthouse, to give an idea of distance, was made out of black rayon and black net with lights of yellow silk embroidered at the top. On the left side of the beach an artificial spray of leaves and berries gave the effect of an exotic tree on the beach, while under the light of the moon sat the hero and heroine. The black velvet Pussy Cat had whiskers from a hairbrush (even my mother with all her zeal would not have cut her own cat's whiskers), beads for eyes and ribbon for a red bow. The owl was made from a snippet of beige fur and for some unknown reason was blanket-stitched round the top. Pieces of the fur were brushed over the eyes, which were two yellow glass beads with brown centres, giving the impression of long, bushy eyebrows. A little piece of bunched-up net contained gold sequins— "plenty of money"— and the honey pot had "Honey" written on it. The guitar had brush bristles for strings. The whole effect was enchanting.

In both these pictures the pieces were sewn on and shapes were cut out with no preliminary drawing.

"Vase of Flowers" (Plate 39), her latest creation, has the joie de vivre of a Matisse. The pieces are attached almost invisibly by nylon thread. The flowers are orange, pink, turquoise and green (two have been taken from flower printed materials) on a yellow silk background. The vase is in silver lamé with gold and silver thread gathered together and a bunch allowed to spring out haphazardly. Black and white lace makes the mat beneath, while black outlines round the flowers and vase add richness. These were partly influenced by Indian embroidery —my mother spent several years in India—which always includes some black for "casting off the evil eye". This picture cost my mother one burnt saucepan as she became too absorbed and the dinner happened to be on at the vital moment of near-completion; but she considered it was worth it as she derived a lot of pleasure during the process of making it. I must add that all her work was completely unaided by me.

My grandmother, Alice Johnson, aged 97, used to enjoy making hats and flowers as a hobby. Not to be outdone with the fabric picture onslaught which had swept the house, she began to make her own design—"A Spray of Flowers" (Plate 41) —by using cherry-coloured ribbons, organdie and some of her original silk and organdie flowers in pinks, yellows, and oranges with artificial leaves added, so that a three-dimensional effect could be achieved. (This idea might be adapted as a jumping-off point for more tentative beginners using artificial flowers and leaves.) She mounted her turquoise blue silk background material over a box, to keep it flat, then set to work pinning all her pieces with small rustproof pins as, although she could read *The Times* from cover to cover without spectacles but with the aid of a magnifying glass—actual stitching was more tedious for her.

Another example of work by an amateur who had had no previous drawing experience was by a primary school teacher who attended a lecture I gave for the London County Council to teachers some years ago. She, in company with the others, was attending an evening course on embroidery in the middle of the term and, like the others, was tired after a hard day's work. The lecture began with a showing of varied examples of fabric pictures, then followed a short account of how to make them and after that the somewhat weary class were to try their hand at doing one of their own. There was a big pile of the most inviting materials, provided by the London County Council, in the centre of the big table round which they were seated. For a time there was an ominous silence and then gradually different members of the class picked out pieces of material that suggested subjects to them and from then on they were cutting away in paper, first mapping out a rough sketch in pencil and eventually cutting out the fabrics. At the end of the course all the pictures were laid out for me to see and it was remarkable what had been achieved, bearing in mind that the class were of mixed ages and most of them had had little or no art training when they were children. The picture I shall always have in mind because it had such impact was entitled "Fire". It had bright red flannel houses with cotton wool smoke pouring from the windows and net curtains fluttering in the breeze, rather reminiscent of a Stanley Spencer painting. In the front, large and looming, head and shoulders only, was a shouting figure with hair streaming in the wind. The cotton wool was the starting off point for this picture!

AN ARTIST

(i) Going to buy a hat at an exclusive Bond Street shop led to a picture of two white pekes looking through a window at six of the spring models. I spotted a gorgeous affair in pinks and cyclamens with flowers and veiling and decided in a rush of extravagance that I must have it. On returning home my husband gave one horrified glance and said "You can't possibly go out in that—we'll have to return it". So back we went and while he was choosing a more suitable and much prettier

42 *Loading Tunny Fish in Brittany:* by Shirley Stone
(*Property of Cambridge Education Committee*)

43 *The Bird:* by Shirley Stone

concoction I was making a sketch of the interior and the shop front. Some weeks later I was commissioned to design a picture using any background but to include two white pekes called Magnolia and Camellia, and I decided that they could be gazing longingly through the window at some hats on stands. The centre ones were decorated with camellias and magnolias, one of the "models" had a small feather from our budgerigar, while others had lace, pearls and beads. The pekes were in white velvet with black bead boot-button eyes. The curtains and pelmet were in pink felt with white gathered net and a blue felt sky was beyond.

(ii) "Double cat" was evolved partly from watching the antics of Dusty, the cat next door, and partly from memories of Picasso's cubist period when he used such things as a violin or a woman's face in such a way that the front, side and back were seen in one picture. "Double cat" was machined in two different coloured nets, one piece in a standing position, the other sitting and each sharing the same head and back leg. Some people interpret this picture as "two cats with one head", and others as "one cat in two moods".

(iii) An unusual and original sight in Chelsea was the man with small trees on a cart drawn by an old horse with a pomeranian standing on his (the horse's) back. I used this against a background composed of a decorative lamp-post with baskets of flowers hanging on it (which I'd seen by the old cricket ground in Sevenoaks), railings and a shop-front with a striped blind.

(iv) The influence of Modigliani's portraits and a model at Goldsmith's College of Art wearing a checked rolled-collar jumper and holding a black dachshund called Harry, against a paisley shawl background, suggested an idea for an etching. This I quickly executed on the spot and later adapted the design for a fabric picture. Black and white cotton squares made the pullover, black wool the hair and I used black velvet for the dog.

(v) The idea for "Cleopatra's barge" came from a children's encyclopaedia. I thought the rams' heads at either end of the boat made a decorative feature. Inside the barge I placed two trees which were typical of the country. Seen in the centre, under pillars topped by lotus-blossom, Cleopatra was placed on her Egyptian couch with a lotus flower in her hand. Beneath the boat were stylized fishes in keeping with the illustrations of small rectangles representing sea under barges and portraying aquatic creatures. The whole design was vignetted against a navy blue woollen background.

(vi) A visit to Battersea Festival Gardens led to "The Fairground", showing a merry-go-round, the big dipper in the background and a stall selling candy floss. The varied patterns and textures seen at a fairground offer a lot of scope. The criss-crossed iron supports of the big dipper are somewhat akin to the huge supports under the piers at Brighton. I placed a couple of old men, slightly Dickensian in flavour, on the left hand side and a girl with candy floss on the right, all showing heads and shoulders only. Boys and girls rode on the animals in the merry-go-round and balloons floated out from the stall. Most of the picture was made out of gaily coloured felts but the pattern on the top and bottom of the merry-

44 *Theatre Box:* by Eugenie Alexander

45 *Dragonfly:* by Eugenie Alexander

go-round was cut from red and white cotton which used these colours for medallion-like shapes.

(vii) A stump-work picture was based on a painting of "Queen Elizabeth I" (Plate IV) which was reproduced in a book I borrowed from the local Public Library. The background was rich gold silk covered in black net, the skirt is of vivid pink velvet with a pale pink, blue and gold design on it (it was fortunate that the pattern echoed the circular quality of the skirt), the sleeves were blue velvet with gold trimmings, the face pink rayon, the hair rust-coloured silk and wool. The shells, braid and heavy black lace, like the majority of the fabrics, are virtually unobtainable now, as they were Victorian and inherited from my grandmother. Pearls, diamanté and the feather in her hand were recent acquisitions, however. The face was worked in a back and a front piece joined together and stuffed with kapok (wool would also have suited the purpose), then under sewn to the background. The other raised pieces were sewn round shapes made by the wool and attached to the yellow silk. Several layers of felt, getting smaller and smaller to give a "built-up" quality, or a papier-mâché mould (made from Copydex and Kleenex tissues) would possibly have been just as effective and far less taxing.

(viii) For some years I had toyed with the idea of doing a box at the theatre and when I was looking at an old magazine I spotted a reproduction of a Victorian print which portrayed Queen Victoria and Prince Albert at the theatre and this inspired "The Theatre Box" (Plate 44). The curtains were of deep rust-red velvet with vivid vermilion pieces of wool for the folds, the front of the box was golden-yellow satin, the wallpaper was striped gold and black silk. The men's uniforms were in varying tones of red rayon, trousers in grey rayon, the women's dresses in pink, purple, red and orange with pink and mauve flowers. The latter had centres of red sequins and pink beads. Gaily coloured garlands decorated the front of the box. Sequins, beads and pearls were used on the dresses, together with black and white lace. Small rounds of lace were cut out for the flowers in one bouquet and variously sized beads were used for another, while one girl carried a fan of black lace. The hair was couched and some French knots were added for ringlets.

CHAPTER VI

Two Fabric Collage Exhibitions

THE Embroiderers' Guild Diamond Jubilee exhibition (including work by amateurs and professionals) presented a new look to embroidery and a large part was played by the ninety-six fabric collages (seven from overseas) which were included. Inspiration for abstract designs was derived from pop art, slabs of cement, drainpipes, cellular structures, cables, planetary shapes, flints, seeds, and glowing embers. A more realistic approach used motifs such as tree trunks, crabs, piers, churches, fishes, landscapes, flowers and birds.

There was a glorious galaxy of colour and tremendous variety of texture in the materials used—fragments of glass, date-stones, shells, wooden beads, gold kid, string, cane, rush, oilcloth and pieces of metal—yarns like mohair, bouclé and Bernat Klein knitting wool. A new spatial quality had been introduced by some works which had been made by drawing threads through holes made in the picture-frames. Then pieces of material were laid over these with the aid of vanishing muslin which was later ironed away. Behind these designs were plain fabric backgrounds. A three-dimensional quality was also very apparent in many pictures with the use of padded suedes, leather, velvet and so on, contrasting with a mixture of flat patterns in the same works.

Variations of tones could be seen not only by the fabrics used but by changes of direction of thread. In some cases embroidery had been blended in to become more a part of the material rather than a sharp contrast. Brightly coloured patterned background materials (squared, flowered, striped and so on) were placed with unpatterned pieces on top using hand and machine embroidery and this was reversing the more usual approach of a plainer background with patterned pieces.

Interesting exhibits included eight panels depicting St Clare (from an original basic design used as a transfer) designed by Margaret Nicholson, who teaches at the Guild, and worked by some of the members. Each member produced her own version of the transfer using different methods of embroidery and varied materials which could serve as an inspiration to Church workers and others, all over the country.

"Three Birds" (Plate V) by Diana Springall had a stained glass feeling with black threads laid across the design and embroidered by hand and machine.

46 *The Jays:* by Eugenie Alexander (*Property of Dr and Mrs Barrie Jay*)

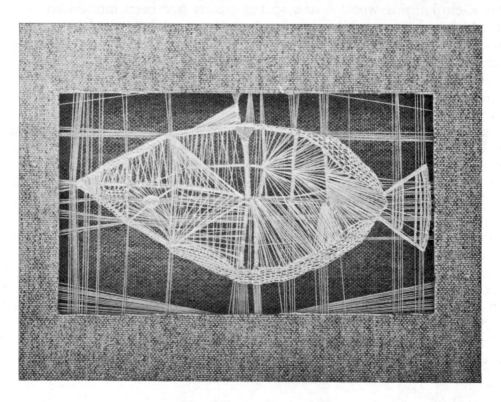

47 *The Fish:* by Mary Stanley

"Flint", an abstract study by the same artist, is an interesting arrangement of shapes in blacks, browns, and dull pinks—with padding, machine and hand stitching.

"King Prawn" by Susan James had a dramatic quality and has been translated into a semi-abstract motif using gold, blacks and greys. It was based on a photograph she had seen and was the first of a series on a similar theme which became more abstract and more raised in surface.

"Fish" by Mary Stanley (Plate 47) was an example of the "spatial" or 3D effect which was achieved by beige linen using threads standing away from the beige hessian background.

The second big exhibition was the competition arranged by Zika Ascher who offered the Ascher award for the best work of art utilizing fabrics in collages and sculpture. The intention was to stimulate artists throughout the world to make greater use of woven materials, and samples from the showroom were made available to those who wanted them. Nearly four hundred different artists from fifteen different countries submitted entries and there was a variety of realistic, abstract, embroidered and glued work. The one hundred collages for the exhibition chosen by the selection committee—Sir Roland Penrose, Norman Reid, Bryan Robertson—were practically all abstract designs which fulfilled such requirements as originality, colour, design, texture and use of fabrics.

The £350 award was given to Enrico Baj for his entry "Lady Sensitive to the Weather" (Plate 48).

He was born in Milan in 1924, studied at the Brera Academy and at the same time graduated in law. He has had numerous one-man exhibitions in Europe, the United States, the Far East, and in London. Raymond Queneau says about his work—"What Baj indicates are secrets—like every painter he alludes, not reveals. He knows perfectly how to balance seriousness and diversion." The illustrated collage is composed of various types of thicker cloth-braids, beads, jewelled eyes and a thermometer in the centre of the face. The colours are in muted browns, greens, greys and black. Parts of the body are highly raised giving a rich sculptural appearance.

"Soumise III" by Hilda Durkin is an arrangement of black, yellow and white lines varying in texture and depth. The curved surfaces are raised to protrude at least 4 inches away from the flatter background.

"Disintegrated Circle" (Plate 49) by June Tiley is in vermilion, ultramarine and white—using rug wools, wooden beads, braids and various embroidered stitches in wools.

"Motif Number 4" by Susan Mary Strutt has a brilliant orange textured background, patterned pieces (predominantly pink) have been machined on to the orange and machine embroidery stitches used.

"Growth" by Angela Sinclair is in oranges, pinks and purples, using "running" machine stitch and hand embroidery.

"Winter" by Geoffrey Evans, a student at Newport School of Art, has padded

48 *Lady Sensitive to the Weather:* by Enrico Baj
(*Ascher Award Winner, 1966*)

49 *Disintegrated Circle:* by June Tiley

crocheted pieces for the cow-parsley—machined organdie clouds—glued seed-pods and beads—it is an exciting and rich picture.

A great many of the entries for the award had been mounted by nailing over wooden "stretchers" used for oil paintings as the fabrics and objects used would have been too heavy for the methods of stretching and mounting I have mentioned in Chapter II.

Authorities Consulted

B. & T. Hughes, *After the Regency* (Lutterworth Press).

Marcus B. Huish, *Samplers and Tapestry Embroideries* (Longmans, 1913).

E. Marx, *Popular English Art*.

Studio Magazine, various numbers.

M. Symonds and L. Preece, *Needlework Through the Ages*.

Victoria and Albert Museum, embroideries, photographs and documents.

Suggested Further Reading

Discovering Embroidery, by Winsome Douglass (Mills & Boon).

Embroidery—A Fresh Approach, by Alison Liley (Mills & Boon).

Your Machine Embroidery, by Dorothy Benson (Sylvan Press).

Singer Machine Embroidery, by Dorothy Benson (Singer Sewing Machine Co. Ltd.).

Decorative Stitching with the Sewing Machine (Needlework Development Scheme, may be obtained from the Embroiderers' Guild—address below).

100 *Embroidery Stitches* (Clark & Co. Ltd., Paisley, Scotland).

Embroidery (published quarterly by the Embroiderers' Guild—address below. (Some of the above may now be out of print, but are possibly still obtainable in libraries.)

* * * * *

Embroiderers' Guild, 73 Wimpole Street, London, W1M 8AX.

Information about membership, subscriptions, etc., may be obtained from the Secretary, Miss Alexandra Beale.